# MENTORING
# — IN —
# SCHOOLS

**Kogan Page Books for Teacher series**
**Series Editor: Tom Marjoram**

# MENTORING
# — IN —
# SCHOOLS

EDITED BY

## MARGARET WILKIN

KOGAN
PAGE

First published in 1992

Reprinted 1992

Kogan Page Limited
120 Pentonville Road
London N1 9JN

**British Library Cataloguing in Publication Data**

A CIP record for this book is available from the British Library.

ISBN 0 7494 0632 1

Typeset by DP Photosetting, Aylesbury, Bucks
Printed and bound in Great Britain by
Clays Ltd, St Ives plc

# Contents

# The Contributors

**John apThomas** is a former primary head, LEA adviser and inspector. He has used mentoring approaches in the induction process for new heads and teachers. He is now attached to the Education Management Centre at Manchester Polytechnic.

**Desiree Back** is the Deputy Head of Soham Village College, Ely. She is currently doing research in the area of school-based training.

**Tom Bailey** is a licensed teacher in the Faculty of Design and Technology at Barstable School in Basildon. He has worked for a number of years in industry where he was involved in the training of apprentices.

**Tony Beck** is attached to the Education Management Centre at Manchester Polytechnic. He has been both mentor and tutor to many colleagues in schools and teacher education, and is currently fulfilling this role on courses in education management.

**Mike Berrill** is Professional Development Deputy at Challney Community College, Luton. He is co-ordinator of mentor training for Bedfordshire and a teacher representative on the National Curriculum Council Task Group on Initial Training.

**Martin Booth** is a lecturer in the University of Cambridge Department of Education and was co-director of a mentor training course.

**Mike Bankin** is the Head of the Faculty of Design and Technology at Barstable School in Basildon and a mentor on the Licensed Teacher Scheme co-ordinated by Anglia Polytechnic.

**Katharine Burn** is Head of History at Cherwell School, Oxford and has been a mentor within the Oxford Internship Scheme for the last three years.

**Barry Featherstone** is Head of the Language Faculty and Co-ordinator of Learning Support at Deacon's School, Peterborough.

**Alison Hill** is Deputy Head at Langley Green First School, Crawley and was formerly Acting Deputy Head and mentor at Waterfield First School, Crawley.

**Susan Holmes** is Head of Modern Languages at Montagu School, Kettering and a mentor on the Northamptonshire Licensed Teacher Scheme.

**Bob Hurst** was formerly Staff Development Co-ordinator at St Peters School, Huntingdon. He is now retired.

**Mike Jennings** is Principal Lecturer in Primary Education at West Sussex Institute of Higher Education where he works on the Articled Teacher programme as a Professional Tutor and is a tutor on the Mentorship programme.

**Mike Kelly** is at the Education Management Centre at Manchester Polytechnic and has a particular interest in the nature and effects of experience-based learning and support for managers in schools and colleges.

**David Kirkham** is Head of English at Newport Free Grammar School, Saffron Walden. For several years he has been a mentor to PGCE students from the Department of Education at the University of Cambridge.

**Bryan Madgwick** is Principal Lecturer in INSET at West Sussex Institute of Higher Education. He is the co-ordinator of the mentorship training programme and works on the Articled Teacher Scheme as a professional tutor.

**Rowie Shaw** has recently been appointed to her second headship at Tong Upper School, Bradford. During 1991 she spent a term as Teacher Associate at the Department of Education at Cambridge University researching on the school-based induction and training of teachers.

**Steve Smith** is Deputy Head and Professional Tutor at Deacon's School, Peterborough.

**Chris Watkins** is tutor to the mentor training course attached to the Articled Teacher Scheme at the Institute of Education at the University of London. He is also Vice-Chair of the National Association for Pastoral Care in Education.

**Margaret Wilkin** was co-director of a mentor training course at the University of Cambridge Department of Education.

# Acknowledgements

I would like to record my sincere and appreciative thanks to all the contributors to this text, who under very severe pressure from many other professional commitments, nevertheless found the time to record their experience and express their views on this important development in initial teacher training.

Margaret Wilkin
February 1992

# Introduction

## THE CHANGING RELATIONSHIP BETWEEN SCHOOLS AND TRAINING INSTITUTIONS

The nature of initial teacher training in the UK has changed radically during the last few years. Professional initiatives and government measures have both contributed to the restructuring of the balance of control and influence in the relationship between training institutions and schools. For two principal reasons, training is moving into schools.

The first concerns the remediation of the 'theory–practice gap' which has so bedevilled initial training over the years. In the wake of the Robbins Report in the 1960s and throughout the 1970s, teachers, tutors and students expressed concern about the lack of continuity between the different forms of knowledge that the school and the college or university department of education (UDE) contributed to training. Two or more decades ago, it was left to the student to undertake as best he or she might the task of integrating the theory provided by the disciplines of education and by methods courses in the training institution, and practice undertaken in school. The potential for integration was not built in to the different elements of training. On teaching practice, students were advised to 'forget all the theory you learn in lectures' because of its apparent irrelevance, and in some institutions they entered schools only for the annual block teaching practice.

Over the years, this separation of theory from practice became less extreme. Well before the intervention of the government in the curriculum of training during the 1980s (see below) it was becoming rare to find the disciplines of education *per se* on the curriculum in a college or a polytechnic. They were presented in a school-focused manner, and the visits of students to schools became more flexible and more continuous throughout the training period. The highly theoretical courses of the post-Robbins era, which had elevated the status of teacher education, had long since been superseded, and modifications to both the structure and the content of the curriculum of training had resulted in more coherent courses in which the school and the training institution components were more fully interrelated.

The second reason for the trend towards school-based training concerns the recognition of the status of teachers as professionals in two respects. First, the right of the teaching profession to share fully in the training of its own recruits is now appreciated. Additionally – due at least in part to the work of sociologists of education during the 1970s and 1980s – the skills that teachers demonstrate in the exercise of their teaching function and their specialist knowledge about classroom practice are now recognised. The main aim of training is that the student or trainee should be enabled to become a good classroom practitioner; the teacher's contribution to this training is not just perceived as valuable, it is regarded as essential.

Of course, teachers have always contributed to training. In supervising students on school placement, they will have given hints and direct advice to their students as the occasion appeared to demand. They may have given demonstration lessons or shared the student's teaching. But it is most unlikely that they engaged in any systematic training. As will be seen from the papers in this collection, that is now changing under the twin influences of professional initiatives and government legislation.

How, specifically and respectively, have the teacher-training profession and the government contributed to this trend towards school-based training?

In 1987, the Department of Educational Studies at Oxford University, together with its associated schools, introduced the 'Internship Scheme'. This scheme is based on the belief that 'teachers in schools [are] best placed to assist the development of young teachers in training' and that 'therefore the course must be school-based but closely coupled to the university contribution which [is] also valuable and distinctive' (Benton 1990, p. 16). Students ('interns') are placed in pairs and in groups of up to ten in one school for nearly two-thirds of the training year. There they work closely with teachers of their subject ('mentors') and under the general supervision of the professional tutor, whose responsibility it is to coordinate training and liaise with the university. The Oxford scheme is unique in the degree to which the training that the student receives in the school and in the university is integrated. Those aspects of the course which deal with classroom teaching matters are jointly planned by mentors and tutors, and tutors visit the schools to work with teachers and groups of students on issues of more general professional concern. The scheme is thus based upon and necessarily depends upon the fullest collaboration between the schools and the university department. Partnership here means a well thought through and principled balance between the contributions of school and university, each of which is considered to be of equal merit.

'The idea of a dialogue between and a synthesis of different sources of knowledge and different criteria for examining ideas and practices is at the core of the internship scheme. It embodies a respect for and a questioning of both the craft knowledge and practical wisdom of practising teachers and also the more systematised and abstract knowledge of university tutors' (McIntyre in Benton 1990, p. 31). Though exceptional in its degree of theoretical justification and in the detail of its planning, the Oxford model of training can be regarded as the extension and culmination of the evolutionary developments referred to briefly above.

Initially, the role of the government was one of confirmation rather than innovation. Circular 3/84 (DES, 1984), issued prior to the introduction of the Oxford scheme, consolidated the general trend – already well established – towards greater cooperation between school and training institution. A close partnership was proposed. This partnership was to include the direct involvement of experienced teachers in interviewing the candidates and in training in the institution, and also in the training and assessment of students in school. School and training institutions were jointly to plan school experience. The circular confirmed that education studies should be concerned with the sorts of issues and problems which the student might meet in the classroom and also that teachers (not yet called mentors) should more actively and purposefully be engaged in their training. The impact of Circular 3/84 was less substantive than constitutional. With respect to the content of training, the characteristics of the more school-based training courses then existing were confirmed as applicable to all, but it was the first time that the Secretary of State had intervened directly in the curriculum of initial training.

In 1988, the Licensed Teacher Scheme was proposed by the government (DES 1988). It was designed to rationalise the various non-standard training routes available to the would-be teacher, but principally to allow the exceptional candidate (the mature entrant wishing to change career or the overseas trained teacher for example) to obtain a teaching post. In this scheme the trainee (licensee) is usually employed by the local education authority (LEA). To be accepted for training he or she must have undergone at least two years of higher education and be at least 24 years of age. He or she usually remains in one school for the duration of the two-year training period under the guidance and instruction of a 'mentor', and after two years is eligible for recommendation by the LEA for Qualified Teacher Status (QTS). During these two years the licensee undertakes such training as the employer deems appropriate in accordance with his or her needs. The nature of the training received by licensees in different LEAs may therefore vary quite considerably regarding the input of the school and of a training institution. In terms of this relationship, the Licensed Teacher Scheme thus differs profoundly from the Oxford Internship Scheme. Not only does the licensee spend almost the entire training period in school, but there is no requirement that the two parties should negotiate and then implement an agreed curriculum in which their respective contributions are equally valued. The criteria for meeting QTS are given in detail, and the courses are monitored and evaluated by HM Inspectorate. That in order to maintain standards in training, schools and LEAs have devised training schemes which do incorporate contributions from a number of sources including institutions of higher education is demonstrated in some of the following papers.

1989 saw the introduction of the Articled Teacher Scheme (DES, 1989a), designed as an experiment in school-based training, but also to combat teacher shortage. The articled teacher, a graduate, enrols in a training institution but is based in school for about four-fifths of the two-year training course. He or she undertakes some off-the-job training. Training is provided jointly by the two types of institution and is negotiated between them and in partnership with the LEA. Like courses in all training institutions, it must meet the criteria established by the Council for the Accreditation of Teacher Education (CATE).[1] Those teachers in school who are responsible for training students (designated 'mentors') usually receive training for this work, although this is likely to vary quite considerably in quality. In this respect, the Articled Teacher Scheme could be regarded as more fully 'school based' than the Licensed Teacher Scheme which does not necessarily provide for such training since training teachers as mentors seems to confirm a more equal distribution of responsibility for the professional development of the student between the training institution and the school. The scheme carries a bursary rather than a grant.

In Circular 24/89 (DES 1989b) the relationship between the training institution and the school has been modified further. It is beginning to become lopsided, with the school as the more powerful partner (Wilkin, 1990). From the point of view of this text, it is an important document in two respects. It acknowledges that if students are to spend a substantial proportion of their training in school, then those teachers who will assume responsibility for them will require 'preparation' for their role (Annex B/1/6). Second, it is recognised that 'school experience should be carefully structured' (Annex B/2/4). This must be a logical step. If schools are to share responsibility for training, then that training must surely be carried out by suitably qualified personnel and must consist of a training programme. But it is suggested that the inclusion of these requirements in the circular signifies and indeed implements the shift from supervision to mentoring. For the school to take some direct responsibility for training (*mentoring*) is very different from *supervising* students who are placed in school in order to put into practice what they have learned in the training institution and whose primary allegiance is to that institution.

In his speech to the North of England Conference in January 1992, the Secretary of State strongly supported school-based training. The speech emphasised the need for a partnership between tutors and teachers which will enable students to link the different aspects of their course. Now 'the college-based parts of teacher training must be fully relevant to classroom practice' (para. 21). In the past, schools taking students on teaching practice remained uncertain about their role in training. It is important therefore that 'schools and experienced teachers involved in training students know what they are supposed to be doing and have the training, the time and the resources to do it well' (para. 17). Thus, in the future, the school is to undertake the mentoring of a student rather than his or her supervision, and the teacher will be trained for this purpose. The mention of the school here, in addition to the teacher, is an interesting development, and the point is reiterated more forcefully later in the speech. It is a necessary inclusion (see the following chapters), but it is also an indication of the extent of the government's commitment to school-based training. There is to be a programme of training to which not only mentors – defined as teachers with a 'real responsibility' for the student's training programme, who are trained for this task – but the school as a whole will contribute.

The consultation document inviting responses to the Secretary of State's initiative was issued soon afterwards (DES, 1992b). It was drawn up by CATE, and in expanding the original proposals, the Council has further demonstrated that in some respects they make sound professional sense. For example, the above proposal to establish a programme of training in the school is now subsumed in a requirement (Annex 1, para. 5) that there should be identification of 'the means by which and the personnel by whom, responsibility will be exercised within the institution and the school' for such elements of the training curriculum as course design, class management, the assessment and recording of pupils' progress and so on. Although 'it is not the intention that institutions will be responsible for "theory" and schools for "practice" (Annex 1, para. 4), this nevertheless indicates that the student's school placement will have to become a structured and purposeful learning exercise rather than an ill-defined experience as it has been so often in the past. The implication of identifying areas of training to be covered and indicating that they are the shared responsibility of both parties is that the school will be taking responsibility for the training of students in at least some of these areas. In others it may be shared. Tutors will be accountable for still others.

From the above brief outline of developments in teacher training, it can be seen that 'mentoring' – that is, the appointment of designated teachers to undertake the training of students in school – has become both a professional and a political issue and, as is implied here, much of what is proposed by the government appears to coincide with current professional aims and practice. Both politicians, and most lecturers and tutors in the training institutions, agree on the importance of a shared responsibility for training. Nor can it be disputed that students should be competent in the classroom on completion of their course of training and 'the value they get out of [the school-based] part of their training is limited if the schools themselves and their teachers do not have a clear role in the training process' (DES, 1992a para. 22).

That the aims of training should be articulated in terms of pre-defined 'outcomes' is not new. For two decades, submissions of courses for validation to the Council for National Academic Awards (CNAA) have very commonly been presented in this form, although the term 'objectives' was preferred to that of 'competences'.

Mentoring is still in its infancy in the UK. Only recently, with the introduction of the Articled and Licensed Teacher Schemes, has it become a matter of urgency that schools undertake a more proactive role in training. Although some schools are going it alone, more usually training institutions and LEAs are cooperating with schools in introducing mentoring. The profession is feeling its way. And because it supports a degree of school-based training, and also because its concern for standards in training cannot be denied, there is a strong commitment to ensuring that any school-based component of training is the best that can be devised. The chapters in this book demonstrate the way in which teachers and tutors are striving to ensure that the training received in school by trainees of all ages is of a high quality. Written before the government's proposals for training and the accompanying CATE document with its draft criteria were announced, they represent the various ways in which tutors, LEA advisors and in particular teachers, have themselves chosen to respond to the need for mentoring under the Licensed and Articled Teacher Schemes and also under pressure of other demands.

# WHAT DOES MENTORING ENTAIL?

What will schools have to undertake if they are to assume extensive responsibility for training as proposed by the Secretary of State? Or even if the requirement is only that they share more fully than hitherto in the training of the student? Their input to training is not specified in the draft criteria for initial teacher training issued by CATE (DES, 1992b). As has already been indicated, who teaches which aspects of the course (within the proposed division of location) is to be negotiated between the two parties. Nevertheless, schools will have to mount training programmes for which they will be accountable. Mentors to undertake these training programmes will need to be selected and trained. Without in any way pre-empting future decisions either at the national or the local level about the form that school-based training should take, this section considers what this might entail for the schools. It draws on the chapters which follow. These are examples of current practice and opinion and represent some of the ways in which the requirements of training in schools might be met. They are interesting for the variation that they display and so are in keeping with the long tradition of diversity in initial training in the UK.

A major question that the schools together with the training institution will need to ask is *What is the role of the mentor?* This is not a simple question! It can only be answered by reviewing the desirable content of training – that is, what it is that the student needs – and then deciding where the various aspects of that training should be located and by whom they should be taught. This is clearly no small task. It is only when this has been accomplished that *mentors can be selected and trained* for their designated tasks.

## The role of the mentor

An indication of what it may mean for the mentor to undertake student training is given in Chapter 2, 'Guidelines for Mentors'. The presentation of the role of the mentor here was derived from the views of teachers on a mentor training course which was designed to enable them to 'take full responsibility' for students in school. As here represented, the mentor either personally undertakes, or arranges for colleagues to undertake, a number of training tasks with the student. These range from devising and implementing an induction programme to attaching the student to a tutor group. There are also proposals concerning the conduct of the mentor when debriefing the student at the weekly meeting, and comprehensive suggestions for the sorts of items mentors might cover when either discussing the planning of lessons or evaluating them. Although the chapter does consider the substance of school-based training to a lesser degree, its primary focus is the procedures that the mentor introduces in order to ensure that training does take place.

The following chapter, 'Establishing Criteria for Mentoring' (Chapter 3) fills out the portrait of the mentor's role. We learn that mentoring is a professional activity. In their meetings, mentor and trainee eschew chumminess: discussion is kept strictly focused and its nature is confidential. The mentor has expectations of the trainee. He or she is expected to maintain a diary and contribute significantly to the work of the department. It is also made clear that the programme of training that the trainee undertakes in school should be staged or developmental and it is the task of the mentor to see that this is the case. This is also a theme of Chapter 11, 'Structured Mentoring and the Development of Teaching Skill'. This is an account of how a school having difficulty in recruiting qualified staff devised its own programme of in-house training for its 'instructors'. The outcome of collaboration between members of staff was a systematic training programme consisting of the procedures to be adopted by the mentor and the substance of mentoring – 12 competences which are classified within four areas and assessed at five levels. Although the complexity and skilfulness of teaching as an activity are acknowledged, the aims of mentoring are limited initially to ensuring that the trainee acquires adequate proficiency in the separate competences which were identified by the staff as 'forming the foundation of a successful teaching career'.

Another way in which the mentor can ensure that the training programme is developmental is through the process of needs analysis. The licensed teacher may enter training with an idiosyncratic life history, yet the mentor must ensure that he or she attains the common standard of knowledge and skills which will enable him or her to be considered for QTS. Chapter 5, 'Assessment and the Licensed Teacher', is an account of how a programme of training is constructed on the principle of regular assessment of the needs of the trainee and subsequent modifications to the training programme to ensure that these needs are met.

So far, only the component parts of the training programme which it is the responsibility of the mentor to arrange have been mentioned. We also need to consider the nature of the interaction between the mentor and the trainee. *How* exactly can the mentor teach the trainee? Several examples are given. Chapter 9, 'Collaborative Teaching', is one account of the mentoring process – a demonstration of a particular mentoring technique, that of sharing the teaching of a lesson. This enables the trainee to acquire initial confidence and also to gain access to the craft knowledge of the subject teacher. Another form of mentor–trainee interaction is discussed in Chapter 4, 'The Nature and Conditions of Good Mentoring Practice'. Here it is suggested that it is the responsibility of the mentor to help the student 'theorise' the classroom; only by relating his or her practice to theory will the beginning teacher be able to provide the best conditions for pupil learning. By drawing on both current practice and more general theoretical domains, the trainee, under the guidance of the mentor, can begin to establish principles of teaching which, being based on personal experience yet also derived from theoretical suppositions, may be perceived as relevant and valuable.

It was indicated above that one task of the mentor (or of the senior management of the school) is to engage colleagues to share in the responsibility of training. Since more of the training period may be school-based in the future, it is possible that the school will have to undertake to train the student in aspects of teaching that are not necessarily directly related to the teaching of a subject and which in the past may have been the charge of the training institutions. This might include what is commonly known as the 'wider professional role' of the teacher: special needs and pastoral responsibilities, the role of governors, and so on. Mentoring cannot be an individual responsibility for the reason that no one mentor will have all the skills and knowledge that comprehensive mentoring of this kind requires. A school-wide climate of mentoring must be established, so that mentoring becomes a general principle which is central to the operation of the school as a community, an activity which will be of benefit to all. Chapter 10, 'Peer Support as the Basis of Good Mentoring Practice' is an account of the development of a learning support team in a school with a high proportion of special needs pupils. It is recognised that as a consequence of this, any member of the staff may at some time or another require additional help and support in the classroom, and is entitled to receive it. The outcome is a 'mentoring school' in which collaborative teaching is regularly employed for the benefit of both staff and pupils. That mentoring is beneficial to all members of the school community is also the conclusion of Chapter 6, 'Can Mentoring Raise Achievement in Schools?' This chapter suggests that many of the skills of mentoring are generic and therefore once acquired by the teacher for the purposes of training the student, can be utilised in the classroom for the benefit of pupils as well.

Finally in this section we return to the fundamental question introduced above. What elements of training are to be undertaken by the school vis-a-vis the training institution? The papers in this collection cannot determine this, but several suggestions can be made. The mentor may undertake some specific methods training (Chapter 9) and also some training in general classroom skills such as the various strategies of teaching (Chapter 3). He or she may also make reference to abstract theory of the kind usually associated with the disciplines of education (Chapter 4). The successful achievement of this depends on the fullest collaboration between both participants in training. Whatever the contribution to training of the training institution in the future, unless the school is fully aware of what this contribution is – and vice versa – the two aspects of the students' professional preparation will not be integrated. There is no chapter in this collection in which any loss of collaboration between school and training institution is envisaged. It is considered that the school should be a 'counterbalance' to the polytechnic which undertakes the teaching of 'relevant and necessary background knowledge' as well as subject methodology (Chapter 3 and also Chapter 1). And the author of the chapter on the most fully developed school-based training programme in this collection (Chapter 11) has a well-defined role for the UDEs, colleges and polytechnics: an engagement in theoretical research which they will then introduce into the schools through on-site tutorials (which presumably could be open to school staff as well as trainees).

The problems of funding and organising such arrangements are amongst the criticisms levelled at the advocates of fully school-based training. Nevertheless, the suggestion that tutors should undertake this sort of role is to acknowledge that their skills and expertise are a necessary element in training if teaching is to remain alive and responsive to the many challenges that confront our schools.

## The selection and training of the mentor

Clearly, the selection and training of mentors cannot take place independently of some notion of what mentoring entails. The mentor must be trained for a specific role and selected as an appropriate person to meet the demands of that role. If the training that the student receives in school is to attract the commitment of student and staff alike, it must appear coherent. This means there must be continuity across the elements of a mentoring system: the role of the mentor including the content and procedures of mentoring, the nature of interaction with the trainee and the assessment of the trainee; the selection and training of the mentor; and the accountability of the mentor. These aspects of mentoring must all be unified and underpinned by a common principle if the practice of mentoring is to avoid being haphazard and is to acquire stability and a sound philosophical base.

But, as will become apparent to the reader, there is no one model of mentoring to which all contributors to this collection subscribe, hence there is unlikely to be any agreement on those qualities which make a good mentor. In Chapter 9, the mentor engages in particular techniques of mentoring, but in Chapter 10, the mentor is primarily a support figure and induction into specific classroom teaching skills is relatively unimportant. Mentoring in Chapter 3 is practical and businesslike (there is a 'contract'); in Chapter 4 it is discursive. And so on. Training to undertake these different approaches to the task of mentoring must necessarily be different. Only if resources of time and money were almost unlimited would it be possible to train teachers in all of these mentoring skills.

That there is likely to be considerable variation in mentor training is amply demonstrated by comparing Chapters 7 and 8. In 'An Experiment in Mentor Training' (Chapter 7), the focus of training is the development of good interpersonal skills. (The importance of these is indicated in the following chapter.) The school mentors (ie, professional tutors, see p. 28) are invited to be open about their experiences and problems. They learn how to interpret conversational responses, how to introduce the notion of personal change, how to act supportively and so on. It is then hoped and anticipated that these skills, which have not only been discussed but also practised in the training sessions, will be useful and used by all in the school context.

Mentor training as it figures in 'Initiating a Mentorship Training Programme' (Chapter 8) is designed to empower the mentor. (Again cross-reference to another chapter is relevant: in Chapter 1, students are shown to prefer assertive mentors.) As in the previous chapter, the aim of training is effective mentoring. But 'effective' here not only embraces the sorts of interpersonal skills indicated above (and also discussed more fully in Chapter 6) but also classroom practice and the design of the student's training programme. The aim of training is the acquisition of certain 'competences' in these and other areas. Yet is it interesting to note that there is little discernible difference between the competences outlined here and the skills described in other chapters in this collection.

The orientation of both of these training programmes can be shown to reflect the contexts in which they were developed. The author of Chapter 7 is the course tutor for the Diploma in Pastoral Care at the University of London Institute of Education, and hence has a particular interest in the quality of interpersonal relations. With respect to Chapter 8, it is suggested that the designation of broadly based skills as competences reflects the fact that the course is award-bearing. Competences are generally considered to be specific and hence relatively easy to define and assess. They are therefore more likely to feature in courses where validation and accountability are important considerations.

## THEORISING ABOUT MENTORING

The above point brings us to an interesting conclusion. It is that the nature of mentor training – and if there is consistency across the mentoring system as defined above, then also of the practice of mentoring – is likely to be a product of the context in which it is developed. These twin issues of context and consistency can best be illustrated by reference to Chapters 2 and 5.

In the mentor training scheme referred to in Chapter 2, mentors were selected by subject for training, and part of their training was practice in the articulation of the principles of teaching their subject. This focus or activity was chosen on the grounds that mentoring was about empowering the teacher to undertake subject methods work with the student. Such an approach to mentoring is particularly appropriate in the department of education at the University of Cambridge where, by tradition, teachers have been given more responsibility for training students than in many other institutions. Moreover, although this is not indicated in Chapter 2, there was no element of training in counselling or other interpersonal skills in this course. While this was not the reason for its exclusion, to have included such a training element would retrospectively have 'contaminated' the purity of the model. In this model of mentoring, the role of the mentor is principally defined as the training of the student in the skills of teaching a subject. Such an orientation to the whole province of mentoring is fully in keeping with the context in which it was developed: an ancient university setting in which the ability of the tutor to convey his or her subject to the student is of principal and fundamental importance. This is an intellectual activity in which the personal relationship between mentor/tutor and trainee/student is of little consequence. Models of mentoring can thus be defined in terms of their underlying and unifying themes. The above model and its component parts can be briefly summarised as follows.

### Model 1: Mentoring as the development of skill in subject presentation

*The role of the mentor in the school:* the major aim of the training programme in the school is that the student should become a good teacher of his or her subject and to this end should have every opportunity to practise the skills which will enable him or her to achieve this goal.

*The selection of the mentor:* according to his/her teaching subject. Personal qualities are relatively unimportant.
*Mentor training:* to include practice in the analysis and articulation of the principles underlying the teaching of the subject.
*Context in which this model was developed:* university.

A very different model of mentoring can be discerned in Chapter 5. As has already been indicated, the task of the mentor here is portrayed as analysing the individual needs of the licensee in order that his or her training may be devised to meet those needs. Once the training programme has been planned, the mentor will continuously monitor the progress of the licensee and where necessary adapt the training programme accordingly. This is a form of mentoring which encourages self-monitoring by the mentor, for if the substance of the training programme is decided by the mentor and his or her colleagues in the school[4] in the interests of the individual trainee, then when a problem arises, the question is 'Where did I go wrong?' If a choice were possible between mentors from the subject department in which the licensee is placed, it could be argued that in this case it should not necessarily be the teacher who is a good exponent of his or her subject but the teacher who displays personal qualities such as the abilities to critically evaluate performance and to be supportive when listening to 'confessions' of anxiety or ignorance, who is chosen for the task.

## Model 2: Mentoring as needs analysis

*The role of the mentor in the school:* the aim of the training programme in the school is to help the 'alternative candidate' gain access to the skills and knowledge of teaching; the means by which this is achieved is the development of the individualised training career.
*The selection of the mentor:* commitment to the notion of open access to teacher training, counselling skills and creativity in planning.
*Mentor training:* devising alternative programmes of training, role plays to improve skills of negotiation.
*Context in which this model was developed:* a shortage of applicants for teaching, one remedy for which was to broaden the recruitment base.

These are only outlines of the ways in which fundamental differences in perspective in mentoring can be expressed. Further such outline models are indicated in the following chapters. For example, Chapter 6 which includes the skills of target-setting and report-writing amongst those required by the mentor suggests a management-skills approach. The model based on the development of interpersonal skills has yet to be developed further. These and many other theoretical matters require exploration and clarification. To what extent is mentoring a reversion to an earlier form of apprenticeship training, as is often claimed? Will there be problems for teachers concerning the articulation of their craft knowledge? What are the intrinsic dangers and difficulties of the mentoring role? Can we in teacher training learn from the mentoring traditions in other occupations? And so on. These broader issues await consideration elsewhere.

We have reached a watershed in teacher training. The days when students on teaching practice were left to find their feet as best they might have long since passed, and the contribution that teachers can make to training is now recognised and acknowledged. Irrespective of the proportion of the training period that is spent in school, there has been a need to enhance the quality of the training received by the student on school placement. These papers show how resourceful and committed to sharing in training schools have become.

## NOTES

1. The Council, which includes teachers and teacher trainers, was introduced at the time of Circular 3/84 in order to establish and monitor standards in training. Its members are appointed by the Secretary of State.
2. Since it was devised by teachers and tutors collaboratively, the Oxford Internship Scheme is taken as representing the profession's vision of school-based training. Since it was launched, other schemes have been introduced elsewhere, but to the knowledge of the writer these have not yet been fully written up and made publicly available. Hence it is difficult to make reference to them.
3. For a full review of school-based initial training see the Report by HM Inspectorate (1991) HMSO.
4. This is of course within boundaries if the goal of QTS is to be achieved. In these models of mentoring, the characteristics highlighted are those particularly emphasised. Of course all mentors will engage analysis of the needs of their students. It is a question of degree.

## REFERENCES

Benton, P. (ed.) (1990). *The Oxford Internship Scheme*, London. Gulbenkian Foundation.

DES (1984). *Initial Teacher Training: Approval of Courses* (Circular 3/84), DES.

—— (1988). *Qualified Teacher Status: A Consultation Document*. DES.

—— (1989a). *Articled Teacher Pilot Scheme: Invitation to Bid for Funding*. DES.

—— (1989b). *Initial Teacher Training: Approval of Courses* (Circular 24/89). DES.

—— (1992a). Speech by Secretary of State to North of England Conference. DES.

—— (1992b). *Reform of Initial Teacher Training: A Consultation Document* (CATE criteria). DES.

H.M. Inspectorate (1991). School-based Initial Teacher Training in England and Wales. HMSO.

McIntyre, D. (1990). 'Ideas and Principles Guiding the Internship Scheme' in Benton, P. (ed) op. cit.

Wilkin, M. (1990). 'The Development of Partnership in the United Kingdom' in Booth, M., Furlong, J., and Wilkin, M., *Partnership in Initial Teacher Training*. Cassell, London.

# NOTE ON TERMINOLOGY

Terminology in the area of mentoring is often confusing. The 'mentor' is the teacher in the school who has direct responsibility for the trainee in the classroom. It is usual for there also to be a member of the school staff (often a deputy head) who has overall responsibility for the organisation of training in the school but who may also participate in training to a more limited degree. This office goes by a variety of names (such as school mentor, general mentor) but is probably most frequently known as that of 'professional tutor'. In order to clarify this terminology for the reader, in the following chapters this term has been inserted where relevant.

# PART I  The Role of the Mentor

## Chapter 1

# Commitment to Mentoring

Desiree Back and Martin Booth

## INTRODUCTION

The importance and role of the school and the practising teacher in the initial training of teachers (ITT) is one of the current concerns in teacher training. This concern is not new but throughout the 1980s it received increasing attention and has come to feature strongly in publications of H.M. Inspectorate and the Department of Education and Science. It gets particular stress in the criteria issued in 1989 by the Council for the Accreditation of Teacher Education (CATE) for the approval of courses of initial training. Critics of the existing system of ITT such as Sheila Lawlor or Anthony O'Hear express an extreme position by arguing that training should be entirely based in the school. Such pressures and arguments have had their effect, and many courses of initial training are being modified or recast so as to give students far more contact with teachers and schools. In some cases, the student no longer undertakes a block teaching practice but spends regular periods of time in school throughout the year. Teachers are serving on advisory committees which oversee ITT courses; they come into the training institution to take seminars or to give lectures; and lecturers are now required to spend time in schools gaining 'recent and relevant' experience of the classroom.

Schools, therefore, are playing an increasingly important part in ITT and student teachers now have frequent and often sustained contact throughout the year with serving teachers. One training institution in particular (the Oxford University Department of Educational Studies) has emphasised the enhanced role of the school by designating those teachers who will have particular responsibility for trainees as 'mentors' – experienced and trusted counsellors who have a teaching, not merely a supervisory role. This is a far cry from the days when training institutions tended to think of the schools as agencies which would provide their students with classes on which to practise their teaching skills. It suggests a radical rethinking of the relationship between the training institution and the school and a need to define and negotiate the distinct and essential contributions both parties have to make to the teaching and training of the student.

## THE SURVEY OF TEACHER AND STUDENT OPINIONS

It is significant that the title of 'mentor' is being used more frequently to describe those teachers who have responsibility for Postgraduate Certificate in Education (PGCE) and other student teachers during their time in school, for it implies their more active involvement in training. It was to explore the views that teachers have of their 'mentoring' role that we conducted structured interviews with subject and senior management teachers in secondary schools in the East Anglian region. Eight senior teachers, six teachers of English and four teachers of history were interviewed, each for about half an hour. We used a structured series of questions which focused on their relationships with students in their schools and the principles underlying their practice in this area. We have also drawn on comments made by 20 English, 13 geography and 12 history student teachers undertaking their block practice in schools in the same region. At the end of the spring term they responded to a questionnaire which explored their views of the guidance they had received. Conclusions based on such evidence are, of course, essentially impressionistic rather than scientific and statistical. Nevertheless, we do feel that our teachers and students raised key issues and highlighted matters which will need to be resolved before effective training can be widely established in schools. The quotations that follow are in general representative of a majority view except where indicated otherwise.

## COMMITMENT TO THE ROLE OF MENTOR

Did the teachers welcome an extension of their role in training? Nearly all the teachers were outspokenly enthusiastic for locating more training in school. In the first instance, they saw the training of students as mainly a practical matter in which direct experience of the school and of the classroom was of paramount importance:

There's nothing like practical experience for learning in terms of teaching . . . looking back on my own PGCE I really found very little value in what I did in college. (deputy head)

I think the best place to learn is actually in the classroom under the supervision of an experienced teacher. (senior teacher)

I think there's a tremendous amount we can do with the students. I feel that sometimes on the PGCE courses they are probably not provided with the sort of practical everyday things that they need to know about before they come into schools. I think we are in a position to see what those needs are more easily than the training institution is – and to cater for them. (senior teacher)

The particular expertise that schools have to offer was stressed:

I personally feel that schools have got a lot of expertise that they can actually feed into the training of teachers . . . I do feel that the school is probably the place where the student is actually going to learn more about what it is like to be a teacher – what the responsibilities are and the implications and so on; teachers have got to realise that they have a big role to play in the development of that . . . I would like to see schools taking a greater part in making suggestions as to what the content of the PGCE should be – what aspects of professional development need to be emphasised, what aspects of theory . . . (head)

And the prospect of closer involvement in initial teacher training was considered exciting:

We feel very excited about the prospects of having a closer relationship with teacher training . . . We want to get involved; we would want to give some of our time, our expertise to that . . . We feel we've got something very positive to contribute to the next generation of teachers . . . (deputy head)

These sorts of sentiments were expressed by most of the group and seem to suggest that in a general sense teachers would indeed welcome a more active involvement in training and envisage that their contribution could be substantial.

A second factor behind such enthusiasm was that the teachers saw such involvement as a new and challenging dimension to their work which would keep them abreast of educational thinking and encourage them to rethink their own practices. In other words, involvement with initial teacher training would bring personal, professional benefits through the need to acquire new knowledge in order to mentor the student effectively or to sharpen practice so as to present the student with the best possible role model. The majority of the teachers we interviewed made such points:

> We see large advantages for ourselves in keeping abreast of what is happening and keeping us fresh in our thinking – having a stimulus coming into the school. (teacher)

> One of the reasons I quite welcome having a student is that it does sharpen your own practice. You know you've got to be doing it right – you've got to be seen to be doing it right – so it does make you think . . . (teacher)

> I think you can become quite complacent as a teacher and roll into your lessons and carry on; but I think if you have got a student you have got to be much more self-aware, self-critical of what you were doing in your lesson and what you wanted the student to get out of it. (teacher)

We asked a teacher of English whether he enjoyed being in charge of students:

> I love it, I love it.

> Interviewer: In spite of the demands and the lack of time?

> In spite of the demands and lack of time . . .

## RESOURCE IMPLICATIONS

Set against this enthusiasm, however, was a clear recognition of the demands which participation in ITT makes on the school. All the teachers we talked to recognised the tension between the training demands of student teachers and the ever-increasing curriculum needs of their pupils. They all felt constrained by the lack of time to talk to students, to observe them as frequently as they would wish and to counsel and guide them:

> On the student's first day in the school I was not free all day – I felt absolutely exhausted . . . You have to try and do a teaching job in the classroom . . . as well as trying to attend to the needs of the student. I felt as if I'd done three days work on that day, trying to answer all the student's questions . . . (teacher)

Senior management was also acutely aware of the added demand of taking responsibility for a student, but saw it in terms of resources and the financial implications for the school, rather than having only limited time available to promote the professional growth of the student:

> Certainly we want to get involved – we want to give some of our time, some of our expertise. But we are aware that there will be a cost involved in that to us and that we shall have to work out the cost implications. (deputy head)

> There are plenty of opportunities here [for school-based training] but it's a two-edged sword because the time that teachers spend with the students has got to be paid for somewhere along the line ... Somehow you've got to have the resources to be able to do the job properly ... There have got to be additional resources for the school to be able to cope with it. (deputy head)

Another deputy put it more bluntly:

> We just can't afford the staffing at the moment to be able to [get as fully involved in school-based training as we would want] – to do a thorough job ... I actually have responsibility for probationers and students and that's just two small parts of the job I do. I'm on half a timetable, or thereabouts – it's usually a bit more – but I find it very difficult to do full justice to the students I've got ... What really concerns me is that there should be time allocated for a member of staff to do this job thoroughly. Under our present staffing figures and the policy the LEA [Local Educational Authority] has, there is just no way we could devote teacher time to doing that sort of approach [fully school-based training].

Our teachers therefore were committed in principle to the more active involvement in training of the school even though they clearly recognised the resource and time constraints.

## THE ROLE OF THE SENIOR MANAGEMENT TEAM

How did the teachers see their roles working out in practice? First, there was widespread recognition that schools will have to reconsider what exactly their role and responsibilities are, and the nature of the training they will be offering students. In all the schools we visited, the Senior Management Team (SMT) had taken a lead in this respect. There was a clear understanding that it was not enough for the SMT to accept student placements on behalf of subject teachers and then to withdraw. The continued involvement of senior management gives credibility to training and offers a shared accountability.

In all but one of our sample of schools, the deputy head takes overall responsibility for students. This extends to acting as a backup to the subject teacher, who despite the best of intentions may find plans to meet the student for feedback and general discussion frustrated by lack of time. Where this happens, the deputy head, who has a more flexible timetable, is able to offer an informed and constructive continuity, thereby reassuring the student that training is regarded as an important aspect of school practice. In this way it becomes something of a 'belt and braces' exercise. No student should be able to say of the SMT: 'They were bound up in their own affairs. I never spoke to the head once.'

If one task of senior management is perceived as ensuring that training does take place, a second is to broaden the substance of that training. In nearly all our sample schools, deputy heads were responsible for introducing the student to the various roles a teacher must undertake as distinct from that of a subject teacher, and to the wider issues arising in school management. Senior management teachers can frequently offer skills with which a subject teacher feels ill at ease. Research indicates that many heads of department, who usually accept responsibility for students, regard themselves as master teachers of a subject, but once they step outside this role, such skills as those of delegation, negotiation and appraisal of other adults cause them anxiety (Bullock, 1988). This was recognised by one or two of our sample:

> I think heads of department in large comprehensive schools are subject specialists and therefore for them, the important thing is their particular subject . . . They're too subject-orientated, too selfish in a way. (teacher)

But new teachers need to be aware of the importance of management issues, for they will be climbing the promotion ladder and may well within a few years be in the middle management tier of a school where management skills will be called for:

> If you have mentors who have not only good classroom practice but also an understanding of the problems of the broader issues of management and can relate these problems to what has to go on in the classroom, then you end up with a better student teacher . . . I would want to focus on middle management. (deputy principal)

A third training task undertaken by senior management is that of offering the student support as a developing practitioner. There were a few schools in which senior management teachers take part in student observation. In one such school in our survey, not only does the deputy head (INSET) observe the student teaching a number of lessons, but the head also observes one lesson at least:

> We like to feel that students feel that they have had a fair deal and that a variety of professionals have an interest in the student practice.

Clearly this has to be handled very sensitively and usually it occurs towards the end of a block of school experience but it can further emphasise the commitment of the school to its training role. It also allows the head personally to assess the student.

A fourth area of responsibility for senior management must be the co-ordination of student training across the whole school. The teachers in our sample were less aware of this need than were the students:

> There were four of us in the same school, and although we were all made very welcome, we all received different treatment. I was lucky; my head of department let me have my head. But another student was in a department only one-man strong, and he was very laid back about the whole thing; two students in the same department were not given much to do; the teachers seemed to want to get on with their own ways and work. (student)

Clearly, there has to be a consistency in the enterprise. The practice of ITT in schools must be systematic. A whole-school policy would ensure that students in the same school do not receive very different standards of guidance. Such a policy gives structure to the obvious enthusiasm and expertise on offer in schools, requiring a genuine shared professional commitment and effective teamwork, agreed objectives and a recognition of the teacher's contribution in terms of time and expertise.

A whole-school policy presupposes a declared agenda, a programme of training to be covered. When prompted, the teachers we talked to indicated that such an agenda might include: typical subject-specific skills, the professional skills of classroom management, discipline, organisation and assessment; cross-curricular themes, dimensions and skills; assessment and evaluation policies, including appraisal; special educational needs; the role of the school in managing its own affairs (LMS); relationships with colleagues as well as with pupils, parents, governors and the outside community.

This is a broad brief. If schools are to take responsibility for structured training in all these areas, clearly senior management will be heavily engaged in the four ways suggested by our respondents above: ensuring continuity; ensuring that training in school remains broadly based and not just confined to classroom matters; demonstrating a personal commitment to the scheme and to the maintenance of standards; and finally co-ordinating policies and personnel.

# THE ROLE OF THE TEACHER

The subject-specific requirements of the training agenda are mainly the responsibility of the subject teachers and include the ways in which a teacher translates his or her specialism into the hard currency of the classroom – that is, the subject craft knowledge necessary for effective classroom teaching. But in addition to the rationale and techniques of subject teaching, the majority of the subject teachers we talked to saw themselves as responsible for promoting student reflection and development within the context of their subject.

> You can say to a student: 'Yes, that's fine. But what about x, y and z? That little group? Did the structure of the lesson allow for them?' That's where the supervisor has a major role to play.

> You must ask the student: 'What are you setting up? What are the pupils actually getting from it? What are they really doing?'

Certainly the teachers see their task as much more than helping students to survive initial teacher training. As one said: 'The student must go on developing concepts and ideas – and it's really an appreciation of the job they've actually decided to undertake.'

At no point must a student be allowed to become complacent, particularly at the end of training when he or she may well have secured an appointment. Most teachers were aware of the need to continue to get students to reflect and to evaluate their practice: 'There is a need to move the students on by showing how they might have done something differently'.

The teachers here are indicating the nature of their involvement in student learning. They do not imply that they didactically direct the student to do x or y. Rather they appear to challenge the student to account for his or her practice, encourage reflection and the consideration of alternatives, and perceive themselves as responsible for helping the student towards a deeper, more sophisticated understanding of the teaching activity. This is a particular form of teaching in which the mentor guides and counsels rather than seeks to impose a viewpoint (although this may be called for at times).

One or two of the teachers we talked to, however, viewed their role in much more limited terms. They saw themselves as assisting a student merely to 'cope' or 'get by'. For them, their task was little more than supervision with little or no teaching of methodology or classroom management involved: 'I'm far more interested really in just sort of seeing how she's coping.' Such an attitude can lead to a cosy atmosphere in which constructive criticism and reflection are absent. As one teacher said of herself: 'If I can use the word to characterise my supervision – it would be maternal. It's a very difficult time for the student, away from college and friends'; and we gained the distinct impression that in one or two cases a 'dependency culture' had been created in which the student appeared to succeed because of the overprotective, oversympathetic mentor. This had been the experience of one student:

> There was no constructive criticism from anyone; I had praise from my college supervisor every time and my mentor was the same. Yet I knew in my bones there must be weaknesses, things I should be doing to improve.

And three of the students who answered the questionnaire indicated how their subject teachers tended to overprotect them:

> [My subject teacher] was a very lovely lady, always positive and encouraging. I don't know whether she sometimes hedged round criticisms of me for fear of shaking my confidence. I never felt underconfident.

> Sometimes I felt she wasn't critical enough.

> I think I should have demanded a broader analysis of my teaching.

This is not, of course, to say that there is no place for support and encouragement.

These few comments can perhaps be taken to suggest that students hope for a professionally critical though supportive relationship with their teachers when on school placements. In other words they would prefer a 'mentor' who would give them direct professional guidance, provide structured opportunities for learning, actively engage in non-threatening evaluative feedback and so on, rather than a 'supervisor' whose task is to ensure that they are happy and that nothing goes amiss – the distinction that is hinted at above.

In addition to promoting the student's professional development the teacher, whether supervisor or mentor, is likely to be required to appraise the student. When asked about this, a few teachers claimed that their practice varies with the type of person a student is, that they have 'hunches' about recognising a 'real teacher' and on the strength of this subjective judgement make decisions about how to manage the training process and how to assess the student:

> There are certain formal things you can do in practice. But I do believe that there is a sort of factor 'x', if you like, which is unquantifiable and at the end of the day, you and I know that this chap, this person, is a teacher.

But hunches are not enough, even though they have a certain credibility for the individual professional. There need to be hard and fast criteria on which a student is prepared for teaching and on which he or she is finally appraised. Specifying such criteria would result in a basic checklist. When asked about a possible checklist or exit criteria, such as is being used by a number of training institutions for grading purposes, there were mixed responses. But the question did prompt some teachers into articulating in some detail what they would look for in a successful teacher: 'I think I'd like it [a checklist], although it would be subjective. On a checklist I would include voice projection, class control and use of resources.' Another, considering the possibility of a checklist, said that in order to pass muster a student '. . . must be well organised, follow the syllabus; prepare lessons and materials and mark books'.

Whereas the above teachers emphasised the practical elements to be included in such a specification, another was more concerned with the philosophical and counselling dimensions of the good teacher:

The perfect teacher for me is a warm and friendly disciplinarian, basing his discipline on mutual respect; the person who realises the aspiration of children; is caring and makes children happy and assists them to enjoy their work.

A substantial number however, felt that a checklist would not be desirable. It was partly that they felt that it would be difficult if not impossible to draw up a list on which everyone could agree, partly that the good teacher was indefinable. At the heart of it perhaps, was the belief that the teacher should be autonomous and no external body should lay down the parameters of the successful teacher:

A checklist would be interesting but no two departments would use it in the same way.

There are basic fundamental points of teaching that you could say a student should be able to grasp and be good at if they are going to pass the teaching practice. But I don't think you can put down hard and fast lists for every individual who comes into teaching.

Despite the reluctance of some teachers to itemise a checklist of exit criteria, we feel it is essential that schools adopt a systematic policy on student assessment, so that students know the criteria against which they will be judged. In this way schools can be fair to all students and can ensure that there is a consensus of all those involved in initial training as to how exactly the commitment to training will be made effective, fair and credible.

# PARTNERSHIP BETWEEN THE SCHOOL AND THE TRAINING INSTITUTION

The teachers to whom we spoke, clearly saw their responsibility for introducing students to the realities of the classroom and of the whole school. Most of them spoke convincingly about the proactive role they were now adopting towards their students, though there was a lack of clarity about the agendas to be covered and about the notion of a whole-school policy on training, thus suggesting the need for training and school development policies.

Where then does this leave the training institution? Do teachers, the mentors of the future, still see a role for it?

Those whom we interviewed were unanimous in their belief that training institution tutors still have an important role to play and that initial teacher training was not something which schools could undertake by themselves. In the first instance, there was an implicit recognition that the tutor from the training institution undertook an arbitrating role, acting as honest broker between school and students should relationships ever break down. But more than this, tutors serve as the link between the higher education institution responsible for the award of the certificate or degree in education and those involved in the delivery of the programme of training. The training institution also is the focus for groups of students in the same discipline, the place where they can get together to discuss and explore experiences – one of the most valuable aspects of any course.

Such arrangements need not, of course, be the exclusive preserve of the training institution; other agencies or people could take over these functions – though it might be argued that they would be less likely to perform them as well as the training institutions, some of which have been in the business of teacher training for well over a hundred years. Where, however, the training institution can make a unique and important contribution to the training process is in providing the theoretical dimension to the practical, school-based activities. That such a dimension was necessary was emphasised by a number of mentors. They clearly felt that students have to have a clear grasp of theoretical underpinning of their practice:

> Without a doubt they do need to spend time on the theory of educational and pedagogical skills – the theory behind what they are doing. (deputy head)

We suggested to this deputy head that the majority of students reject the theoretical elements of the course, believing that theory provided little practical guidance. He replied:

Ah well, it must; the theory has to be related to the practice and not the practice to the theory. I think it's very important to assess the effective nature of the theory we give these embryonic teachers. If it helps them to understand the situation they are in, helps them to understand relationships and the way things evolve and helps them to develop then that's probably the right way . . .

A head echoed this in saying: 'Theory must be born originally of practice; practice itself has constructed the theory.' These comments seem to indicate that though they believe that the student must start with the realities and practicalities of the classroom, the principles underlying such practice must later be addressed.

A teacher of geography explained what he felt was the particular contribution of the training institution lecturer by instancing a particular area:

University tutors can help with the theoretical background, for instance, with the use of language and its relationship to learning – why we are using certain types of language, group work, discussion work – that kind of thing. I think in a way some teachers when they have been teaching a few years know the good practice – but it's quite interesting to have that unpacked and put into a theoretical mould by the lecturer.

Yet another teacher referred to the research which training institutions are engaged in which can give a credibility and breadth of vision and understanding to the process of education which the schools are unable to provide. Another spoke interestingly of the seeds which had been sown in the lectures he had heard on the philosophy of education:

I found after ten years in teaching these were the things that I turned to more and more.

Interviewer: In other words, seeds which have been planted during that training year . . . began to develop later. Isn't there a danger then if we get fully school-based training that part will be completely phased out?

I think so. I think there will be a danger that you will get a small group of educationalists who become more and more remote from the process of education. It is important that our philosophers are also in touch with those who are directly involved in the process . . . I went back and did an education philosophy course after ten years of teaching and I found it did a lot more than just recharge my batteries. It focused my thinking –

a recognition that some of the courses students may follow in their initial training course may well not bear fruit until later in their careers.

So there was a clear recognition that there are broader, more theoretical dimensions to training which schools would feel uncomfortable in taking over.

## CONCLUSION

Training is a co-operative venture but the nature of that co-operation is changing. Among the teachers in our sample, there remained vestiges of the old belief that simply placing students with practitioners and talking to them about their teaching is sufficient to ensure that they will be inducted into the profession. But by far the majority of teachers indicated that they participated actively in training, that they were mentors. They provide a context of facilitating and supportive guidance which both permits and encourages the student to reflect, to consider alternatives, to become self-aware, to respond to challenges, and in so doing they are facilitating the student's ability to articulate his or her practice and so to review that practice constructively and rationally.

This limited survey suggests, however, that although teachers may be demonstrating the skills of mentoring, they may not be confident about the areas in which these skills are to be exercised. In effect the training programme in the school tends to remain unarticulated and uncoordinated. That so many of the teachers had to be prompted to suggest the substance of the school role in training implies that there may be quite some way to go yet before they feel fully empowered as trainers of teachers.

The teachers recognised that in schools there is an inevitable tension between mounting a coherent programme of training for the student and the curriculum needs of pupils. Teacher training in schools must inevitably be adapted to the curriculum that the pupils are following. It also has to be tailored to the staffing, time and resources available. It may not be possible to implement a planned series of classroom activities because it does not coincide with the way in which the curriculum is being delivered. Or the programme may have to be interrupted or adapted because of the general school programme of exams, work experience visits and so on. The training institution on the other hand is free to devise 'ideal' teaching situations unaffected by such considerations. For example, within subject studies, time can be given to the range of ways in which it would be possible to meet the requirements of the National Curriculum. To build up in a coherent and progressive manner the sort of knowledge and skills that students will later be able to use with their pupils is of course the function of the training institution. Nevertheless, tension between the training institution and the school may arise because the models provided in the former are constrained by the circumstances pertaining in the latter.

The crux of the matter is the liaison between school and the training institution. Both parties must work together to create an overall programme of training where theory and practice mesh and complement each other, where roles and teaching areas are both negotiated and where the notions of professional development and clearly defined targets are to the fore. We have suggested in this chapter that there is considerable enthusiasm for developing this partnership – an encouraging foundation on which to build initial teacher training in the future.

## REFERENCES

(The place of publication of books is London unless otherwise stated.)

Bullock, A. (1988). *Meeting Teachers' Management Needs* Norfolk: Peter Frances.
DES. (1989) Circular 24/89. *Initial Teacher Training: Approval of Courses* [the CATE criteria] DES.
Lawlor, S. (1990). *Teachers Mistaught: Training Theories or Education in Subjects* Centre For Policy Studies.
O'Hear, A. (1988). *Who Teaches the Teachers?* Social Affairs Unit.

*Chapter 2*

# Guidelines for Mentors

Bob Hurst and Margaret Wilkin

## CONTEXT

Research evidence suggests that in the past many teachers have been in some doubt and confusion about their contribution to initial teacher training (ITT). They have not known whether they were supposed to teach the student directly (and if so what) or whether their role was merely to keep an eye on him or her, give the occasional hint or tip when things went a bit wrong and in general ensure that all was well. That they lacked this sense of direction in their role as guardian or supervisor reflected the relationship between schools and training institutions – a 'partnership' in which the training institutions were dominant and the contribution of the schools to training neither clarified nor fully acknowledged.

These are generalisations of course. There will have been colleges or university departments where the training relationship with the schools was well thought through, where the work undertaken by the student in school and college was integrated and formed a coherent programme of training, and where the skills that teachers can bring to student training were explicitly recognised and incorporated into training in the form of a well-defined and negotiated tutorial role. But undoubtedly this was the exceptional rather than the usual state of affairs.

Things are very different now. Innovative courses such as that at Oxford University Department of Educational Studies have changed the climate of training, and recent government initiatives have hurried things along. The traditional relationship between schools and UDEs and colleges has been challenged and is now in the melting pot. But one thing is certain. In the future, schools will have a much more active part to play in training. The extent to which this is the case varies and will probably continue to do so, for although the framework of training prescribed by the Council for Accreditation of Teacher Education (CATE) has introduced a uniformity hitherto unknown in traditional courses across training institutions, in the Licensed and Articled Teacher Schemes there are alternative forms of training which are a further variation on the balance between the respective contributions of training institution and school.

All of this does not mean that schools wish to assume, or feel that they are capable of assuming, complete responsibility for training. In the professional community it is rare to find support for this point of view – the principal function of schools is to educate the young and must remain so. It does suggest that a transformation of roles is taking place.

Given this situation, how is this transformation in the role of the teacher to be introduced? Clearly one imperative is that teachers should feel competent in their new partnership role. They must know the aspects of training for which they are to be accountable and be confident that given the resources, they can deliver them. In short they must feel empowered.

This was the background to an in-service mentor training course run at the Department of Education at the University of Cambridge (CUDE) between 1987 and 1990 which was attended by a total of 63 teachers from secondary schools in 5 LEAs. The tradition at CUDE has been for tutors to undertake relatively limited visiting of students in school. Hence the aim of the course was to 'enable the teacher supervisor to take full responsibility for the professional development of the student during the teaching practice term'. By definition this was to include responsibility for training, not merely in the skills of classroom organisation and management, but in subject teaching too. If the student is to spend long periods in school and if this most fundamental goal of training is not to be neglected, then the school must share this training task. The annual course was of approximately 30 hours' duration (including a residential week-end) and the teachers attended by subject. It was funded by the LEAs, Cambridgeshire being the principal funding body.

With a few exceptions, the teachers on the course were senior members of school staffs who had for several, sometimes many, years been supervising CUDE students and who had liaised closely with their respective methods tutor in the UDE (who also contributed intermittently to the course). They were therefore highly experienced and well qualified in the matter of student supervision, but exactly what 'supervision' entailed for each member of the group and to what extent they shared a common vision remained unknown.

A first step in the process of empowerment is the articulation and hence the acknowledgement of the relevant expertise that one already possesses. Not only is this confidence-building but it provides a basis for further development. We all have skills which remain unrecognised by ourselves and others because they have become routine practice over the years and are no longer perceived as skilful, or because the context in which they might flourish is denied us. This is as true of teachers in their teacher training capacity as it is of academics in a context of reduced resources for research and publication. In the matter of preparing for where we are going, rather than setting targets with little reference to our current position, it is easier and more rational to clarify where we are now, to review that position and to generate recommendations for future practice from it.

With this in mind, the teachers were invited, as a course exercise, to discuss and note down how they perceived their relationship with the PGCE students in their charge. In their accounts they were invited to include anything they wished – training activities that they personally undertook with the student, or that were undertaken by the school as a whole, comments about attitude, about accountability, about assessment and so on. Their views were then collated and returned to them for refinement and confirmation before being reproduced in a booklet: *Guidelines for Mentors and Supervisors* (CUDE, 1990) which was then accepted by Cambridgeshire LEA for use in schools where this was felt to be appropriate.

A word about methodology. The distinction (above) between actual practice and ideal practice was difficult to maintain. In the first place the initial request to the teachers contained a tension. To suggest that they note down what they do in order to contribute to guidelines for supervisors represents an incompatible requirement. The term 'guidelines' suggests an ideal code of conduct, yet daily practice may be far from 'ideal'. It may be constrained by all manner of problems – lack of time, illness, pressure of other demands, and so on. In addition, if one is asked to record what one *does*, unless there is a specific and heavy emphasis on being absolutely accurate (which there was not) there is probably a natural tendency to represent one's actions in a positive light, particularly if one is with a group of one's peers. This may mean no more than recalling that one 'usually' does 'x' or 'y', although it has not been possible for the last two weeks, or that one intends to do 'z' regularly but in the end only manages to do it occasionally. The distinction between ideal and actual behaviour is not always easy to establish. In the end, as will be demonstrated below, the guidelines came to represent an ideal code of practice without our having consciously passed from the stage of 'This is what we do now or have done in the past' to 'How can we improve our practice? What do we think we should try to do in the future?'

It should be remembered that the teachers' views as encapsulated in this document, were the outcome of relatively leisurely and unconstrained discussion. They are the views of experienced student supervisors whose schools have had long-term association with CUDE. This means that the recommendations are likely to be comprehensive, as indeed they are, since there was time for the teachers to review their practice and they were able to draw upon a considerable accumulation of experience. The number of participants (63) seems to have been a less important influence here than might be imagined since there was considerable duplication of items across teachers irrespective of subject or of status.

## THE GUIDELINES

The *Guidelines* therefore consist of the teachers' own views of their relationship with their students. The presentation is user-friendly and there are 7 sections:

1. Relationships with the Training Institution
2. Relationships with the Trainee
3. Induction and Planning a Programme for the Trainee
4. Observing the Trainee
5. Conducting a Debriefing Discussion
   i.   general procedures
   ii.  the general-skills agenda
   iii. the subject-specific agenda
6. The Wider Professional Role of the Trainee
7. The Assessment of the Trainee

Each Section is headed: 'It is suggested that the mentor or supervisor should . . .' and there follows a list of recommendations:

1. Relationships with the Training Institution
It is suggested that together the school and the training institution should:

- ensure that all communication is clear, comprehensive and prompt;
- establish a partnership between mentor and university or college tutor such that each makes known to the other his or her professional expertise and needs and similarly recognises those of the other;

- discuss what the school might reasonably and in general expect of the student in terms of his or her professional development;
- ensure and welcome regular visits to the school throughout the trainee's placement by staff from the training institution who are known to the trainee;
- fully inform each other of any relevant information concerning the trainee;
- ensure that there is agreement on the procedures for dealing with the trainee who has severe difficulties of any kind.

2. Relationships with the Trainee

It is suggested that the mentor or supervisor should:

- remember that the trainee is the supervisor's responsibility and that time must be found to give to this commitment;
- accord the trainee the respect due to a fellow professional and reciprocally expect professional standards from him or her;
- ensure that relations with the trainee are governed by an awareness of his or her needs;
- be readily accessible and be willing to be a counsellor to the trainee as well as a mentor and an assessor.

3. Induction and Planning a Programme for the Trainee

It is suggested that the mentor or supervisor should:

- recognise that a well-devised induction programme is essential for the trainee's sound professional development;
- regard any preliminary visit(s) as part of the induction programme and plan it/them accordingly;
- brief the trainee on the resources available and provide him or her with all the texts and documentation necessary for teaching the curriculum. The mentor or supervisor should talk these through with the trainee;
- give the trainee some indication of the levels of attainment and the behaviour patterns which he or she may expect of particular classes;
- inform the trainee of school and departmental policies and procedures on matters of discipline, safety and special needs;
- provide opportunities for the trainees to observe other teachers who have a range of teaching styles and who teach both within the department and also in different subject areas. These should continue throughout the term and the views of the trainee on these lessons should be sought and used as a resource in the trainee's own professional development;
- devise a phased and suitably paced introduction to teaching

appropriate to the individual trainee's skills, confidence and interest. This should include opportunities to assist in classes before taking full responsibility;

- not necessarily expect the trainee to undertake a full teaching timetable even towards the end of the school placement;
- transfer responsibility to the trainee with tact, conviction and certainty. When the trainee is in charge, the teacher should redirect to the trainee any questions, appeals or references directed to him or herself;
- provide the trainee with opportunities to work in partnership with another trainee;
- provide opportunities for the trainee to team teach with an experienced teacher;
- set aside a time each week for all trainees placed in the school to meet for discussion either with or without the co-ordinating teacher appointed by the school;
- not necessarily expect the student to teach either those pupils who are regarded as 'difficult' or of low ability, but where such teaching commitments are undertaken, should ensure that the trainee receives full support and appropriate guidance;
- not be a probationer.

## 4. Observing the Trainee

It is suggested that the mentor or supervisor should:

- at all times be aware of the importance of being sensitive and impartial when undertaking observation of the trainee;
- review the lesson plan before observing the trainee teach;
- consider beforehand how the trainee is to be observed and should ensure that observation of the lesson is undertaken in a disciplined, focused and accountable manner;
- observe, and in the post-observation debriefing, comment upon both the lesson as a whole and also specific aspects of the lesson . . . but –
- discuss with the trainee beforehand what is going to be the main focus of observation;
- give the trainee some immediate feed-back after the lesson, even if only for a few minutes;
- at the start of the school placement allow the trainee to choose which lessons are to be observed;
- ensure that the teacher whose classes the trainee is taking observes him or her teach at least once a week;
- arrange for other teachers in the department or even of other

subjects to observe the trainee and contribute their comments in the post-observation discussion;

- from time to time report back to the head of department on the observed lessons;
- observe and subsequently comment upon (see next section): the general teaching skills of the trainee and the subject-specific skills of the trainee (see below).

5. Conducting a Debriefing Discussion (general procedures)
It is suggested that the mentor or supervisor should:

- arrange a regular, formal, weekly meeting with the trainee of at least a period in length. The mentor or supervisor should seek to be timetabled for this responsibility;
- be available when required by the trainee for additional informal meetings;
- be prepared to devote considerable time, initially at least, to discussing with the trainee the preparation and evaluation of a lesson;
- ensure that the trainee is aware of the professional responsibility of maintaining both planning and evaluation records of his or her teaching. The trainee's file or teaching record should be readily available and should be kept up to date;
- review the trainee's file regularly and be aware of its importance as a resource during the pre-lesson discussion and post-lesson evaluation.

During the discussion, it is suggested that the mentor or supervisor should in general:

- encourage the trainee to review and reflect upon his or her practice and so to advance his or her professional development. The attitude of the mentor should support the trainee and a sense of progression should be fostered;
- encourage the trainee to develop professional independence and make known to him or her that mistakes are learning experiences;
- decide beforehand which response style is most appropriate for the circumstances but be alert to the need to change style if the response of the trainee suggests that this might be desirable;
- regard the agenda of the discussion as flexible in order to allow for the individual needs of the trainee;
- engage in constructive evaluation of the trainee's practice rather than critical assessment. All formal meetings should end positively;
- having made notes when observing the trainee, use these notes as

a basis for discussion during the meeting. The trainee should be given a copy of these notes;

- cite evidence to support comments on the trainee's performance;
- recognise that the insights which emerge during discussions of this nature with the trainee also provide an opportunity for further professional self-development and that assuming responsibility for a trainee is therefore a mutually beneficial exercise.

5. Conducting a Debriefing Discussion (the general-skills agenda)
It is suggested that it is the task of the mentor or supervisor to promote the development of the trainee selectively in:

- the preparation of lessons and teaching material:
  are the aims and objectives of the lesson appropriate? Is the material suitable for the range of abilities within the class? Is it integrated with previous lesson topics related to children's own knowledge and experience? Is the material well structured? Is the planned used of resources creative and likely to motivate? Is there sufficient variety of teaching method to maintain interest? Does the planned use of materials take account of cultural background and gender issues?

In a similar vein, detailed suggestions follow, for lesson participation, taking a lesson, classroom management, presentation of self, relationships with the class, language skills, assessment, and dealing with homework.

5. Conducting a Debriefing Discussion (the subject-specific agenda). An example: in history it is suggested that the mentor or supervisor should evaluate and develop the trainee's ability to:

- plan a sequence of lessons using a theme, topic or period;
- make use of a range of historical sources such as pictures, documents, and artefacts, and to have a clear understanding of the reasons for using the chosen sources (eg evidence or illustration);
- encourage in the children a questioning attitude with respect to the possibility of bias, selective reporting and a lack of reliability in historical evidence;
- develop children's empathetic understanding (eg with respect to the intentions, motives and actions of those who lived in the past);
- distinguish in the presentation of material between cause and consequence, change and continuity;
- use historical concepts precisely and develop within the children a similar respect for the exactness of such terms (eg 'revolution' or 'imperialism');

6. The Wider Professional Role of the Trainee
It is suggested that the mentor or supervisor should:

- introduce the trainee to departmental and other colleagues and invite their co-operation and help in sharing responsibility for him or her;
- arrange for the trainee to spend time with the head of department (where these two roles are not coincident);
- encourage the trainee to contribute responsibly to assessment in co-operation with the teacher concerned;
- make arrangements to attach the trainee to a tutor group. The trainee should be encouraged to assume pastoral responsibilities to go to parents' evenings;
- encourage the trainee to participate in extra-curricular activities;
- expect the trainee to share duties with a teacher, including participating in school trips;
- offer the trainee the opportunity to attend any suitable in-service courses or meetings;
- provide an opportunity for the trainee to become acquainted with the careers service offered by the school;
- either personally, or invite a colleague such as the deputy head, to brief the trainee on outside agencies and their functions, and inform the trainee of important developments within the education service.

7. The Assessment of the Trainee
It is suggested that the assessment of the trainee should take the form of a profile:

- which should be a continuous record of the trainee's development as a practitioner throughout the period of the school placement;
- in which the meaning of the terms used should be mutually agreed by trainee and mentor or supervisor;
- which should contain a number of sections concerning different aspects of the trainee's developing professionalism (eg experience, achievements, skills demonstrated, future training needs);
- which should include opportunities for self-assessment by the trainee;
- which should be open and negotiable. The trainee should have full access to all assessment procedures and documentation;
- which should be regarded by both trainee and mentor as an aid to professional learning rather than just an evaluative exercise.

## A SENIOR TEACHER'S OBSERVATIONS ON WORKING WITH THE *GUIDELINES*

Our school was one of those invited to participate in the Cambridge-shire Articled Teacher Pilot Scheme. An audit was undertaken to assess the preparedness of staff and school for the responsibilities of receiving and training three or four articled teachers. The basis of this audit was the document *Guidelines for Mentors and Supervisors* produced by CUDE in association with PGCE student supervisors. This document was chosen since many of its recommendations had already been put into practice in the school. Three of our heads of department had participated in the in-service course and their ideas had been incorporated into the school's trainee supervision policy before the publication of the *Guidelines* document. We assessed our performance as PGCE supervisors/mentors in the light of the *Guidelines'* recommendations and discovered, as expected, weaknesses as well as strengths.

The greatest responsibility for supervision at PGCE and articled teacher level is borne by the subject mentor who has day-to-day oversight of the trainee's classroom experience. The review and discussion of lesson planning, the evaluation and debriefing which follow a lesson observed, these, subject mentors claim, are the most important contributions to the trainees' development. Through one-to-one discussion, content, teaching and class management skills are analysed.

Not all mentors pronounced themselves satisfied with their performance in this crucial role. The pressures of the timetable afford little opportunity for debriefing at the end of a period when the triumphs and disasters of a lesson are still tangible. The noise of the next class assembling in the corridor is an inhibiting background to reasoned conversation. Postponing the discussion leaves scope for reflection, which some mentors prefer, but also eats into non-teaching or after-school time when most heads of department have other responsibilities to discharge. Several reported that their debriefing sessions were perfunctory and that in-depth discussion was always deferred until the weekly meeting. Others with more favourable timetables found time for regular planning and debriefing or delegated some of this procedure to other departmental colleagues. Having to share the responsibility for student training in this way can be regarded as a bonus rather than a problem, however. Provided that those concerned liaise thoroughly and agree on the form that the programme for the trainee should take (ie that they do not convey contradictory messages to the student) it may be beneficial for the student to have the opportunity to work closely with more than one teacher and so broaden his or her knowledge of classroom techniques. Nevertheless, it is clearly the timetable, not some concept of good practice, which is a major determinant of when discussions with the student take place and how effective they may be. The extent and depth of the teaching of the student that the mentor can undertake is conditioned by the day-to-day pressures of school life. We must face the fact that the enhanced contribution of the school to teacher training means that additional resources, especially time, must be allocated to mentors.

Significantly it is through planning and debriefing that 'supervision' becomes 'mentoring', for mentoring implies involvement with the learning process of the student, supervision merely 'keeping an eye on the student'. Mentoring means discussing a lesson plan with the student examining its subject content, its relevance to the scheme of work, the variety of teaching techniques by which the material could be delivered and so on. Furthermore, the planning and delivery of the lesson should be seen in the context of the trainee's development. Content and technique displayed in week 2 of the school placement ought to be better focused by week 10. The ability to monitor the trainee's progress is implicit in mentoring. That this developmental dimension of student learning in school is only mentioned in the most general sense as a heading in the *Guidelines* is a weakness of the document. It features as a phrase in the heading of Section 5 (ii) ('It is suggested that it is the task of the mentor or supervisor to promote the development of the trainee selectively in') where its impact is lost. Clearly this is an essential component of the teacher's task with respect to the student: to ensure that the student's skills and understanding of the art and craft of teaching are being steadily enhanced during the time spent in school.

In a more general context the *Guidelines* refer to 'Induction' and the 'Wider Professional Role of the Trainee', areas for which the professional tutor rather than the subject mentor is responsible. In general, induction will consist of familiarising the trainee with the procedures, policies and resources of a school. But the *Guidelines* go further in suggesting that the trainee be given opportunities to observe other teachers who have a range of teaching styles and who teach both within the department and also in other subject areas. Such opportunities are not just valuable, they are essential, particularly for the articled teacher. One can too easily be engaged by the personality and presentation skills of an experienced teacher which may obscure what the trainee ought to be registering: class management technique, matching style and lesson content to the ability of the group, adaptability to class and individual response involvement of the whole group, in fact those elements of a lesson which the mentor seeks to pin-point when evaluating the trainee's teaching. Observation is a training activity which we have undertaken in the school for some time.

Experience of the tutor group as distinct from the class situation is a generally accepted recommendation which the school has always implemented for its trainees. But attachment to a tutor group can be a barren and sometimes demoralising experience unless the purpose and philosophy of the school's pastoral/pupil support system is made clear. The relative informality and variety of relationships between a tutor and his or her tutor group make it difficult for a trainee to become involved and there is usually insufficient time for the tutor to explain the complex relationships which a group embodies. The onus is on tutors (this having been negotiated by the mentor) to make sense of this experience for the trainee, just as the student will need help to make sense of the observations which he or she undertakes. Although our teachers strive to do this for their students, this important responsibility is not mentioned in the *Guidelines*.

In discussing the wider professional role of trainees the *Guidelines* suggest that they should be briefed about current educational issues which affect the whole school. We agreed that our record here was good, since we had met this recommendation for many cohorts of students. The school has regularly drawn up for its trainees a programme in which senior staff discussed with them such matters as records of achievement, student-centred learning, assessment procedures, teacher appraisal, and so on.

The school's most obvious asset in seeking to implement the *Guidelines* is the experience of its mentors. Our audit revealed that six departments had been receiving trainees for at least ten years, three others for a shorter period. All were committed with some reservations to the ideals which the *Guidelines* set out. When the *Guidelines* were discussed by mentors they were accepted as a counsel of perfection, an ideal, of which many would fall short. As the responsibility for teacher training moves more towards the schools it will be a sound framework on which the new structure of teacher education may be built. All our mentors affirmed that pressure of time in school and the short-term nature of teaching practice were the obstacles which stand in the way of a closer approach to the ideal. Those who are about to become mentors of articled teachers have welcomed the time-scale and flexibility which the new arrangement brings. The longer trainees are in school the closer we shall get to a comprehensive implementation of the *Guidelines*.

## COMMENTARY

What do these *Guidelines* say about the teacher's role in training? There can be no doubt that the teachers who proposed these items have a powerful vision of the schools' contribution to training. Nor can there be any doubt that for a teacher to undertake the range of training activities indicated here would be very demanding indeed, particularly in view of the other pressures that teachers are currently subject to. The overall training that the student would receive, were the *Guidelines* to be implemented, would certainly be comprehensive, and all of this very extensive training agenda is to be either arranged or personally undertaken by the subject-teacher directly responsible for the student. There can be no mistake. Undertaking the task of training students in school is no sinecure!

According to these *Guidelines* then, the role of the teacher and the school is to provide the student with a wide range of opportunities for professional development, and that is of course the function of the school placement. What is not always evident to the reader of this document is how these opportunities are to be interpreted. In other words, here is a structured framework for training, much of which consists of proposed procedures, which are in many cases (although certainly not all) devoid of content. To take an example: 'It is suggested that the mentor or supervisor . . . provide opportunities for the trainee to team teach with an experienced teacher' (Section 3). The reasons or justifications for proposing this ('in order that the student may learn to do "x" or "y"') have not been specified. Another example: '. . . encourage the trainee to participate in extra-curricular activities' (Section 6). Why this is a good idea is not stated.

This is both useful and interesting. It is useful because it broadens the applicability of the *Guidelines*. It means that they can be used by teachers and tutors who hold rather different ideas about the underlying principles and practice of teaching and hence of training. For example, in the general-skills agenda (Section 5) concerning 'the preparation of lessons and teaching materials', the teacher is invited to promote the development of the trainee selectively in a number of areas: the structuring of teaching material, the variety of teaching method and so on. But nothing is said about the way in which materials *should* be structured, and no particular teaching method is recommended. These *Guidelines* therefore have the advantage that they can accommodate a variety of theories of teaching while at the same time, because of their comprehensive nature, help to ensure that the student receives a coherent and broadly based training in school.

However, this 'omission', if it can be called that, is interesting for another reason. And here we return to the theme of empowerment. It could be argued that had the teachers concerned felt fully empowered in their role as trainers of students, then there would be more *explicit* evidence that they do more than provide these opportunities for trainee development. The ways in which those opportunities were used would also have been (confidently) stated. There can be no doubt whatsoever that the teachers who contributed to the *Guidelines* play a mentoring role. It would not have been possible to have drawn up such a diverse yet comprehensive training programme had they been merely supervisors in the strict sense of the term. Supervisors would not even have been aware of these opportunities for student training. But that the substance of the mentoring role remains implicit for much of the time, seems to suggest that the mentoring role has yet to be confidently and conspicuously *lived*.

There is an important exception to this, however. Although there is very little indeed about the nature of mentor–trainee interaction, there is a major reference to this in Section 5. It is suggested there that the mentor should adopt a particular stance towards the student – that of supportive facilitator rather than, say, didact. Is it possible to suggest from this one example that this is how this group of teachers perceive the actual process of mentoring?

What do the *Guidelines* say about the role of the school in training? Since the teachers were asked only about their own role, and not specifically about that of the school, it is necessary to look for an implicit rather than an explicit response here. However, there are a number of items which refer to other colleagues in various capacities and which are sufficient in number to indicate that in the opinion of the teachers on this course it is the responsibility of the whole school to support and share in the training of students.

The *Guidelines* clearly suggest that in the interests of providing the student with the best possible in-house training, the teacher hopes, even expects, to be able to call on the help of colleagues, not just in the same department (which might be relatively easy to arrange) but also in other subject areas. These colleagues are to be invited to contribute in a range of ways – by being the focus of observation and subsequently attending any follow-up discussion, by contributing their particular expertise where the teacher lacks that specialist knowledge, by inviting the co-operation of the student on pupil assessment and so on. In addition, accommodation is to be found (sacrificed?) for debriefing sessions and also for students' weekly meetings. Thus training the student in the school is not a one-person task. It is assumed that it is a whole-school responsibility. Although there is no mention here of the role of school management in co-ordinating the various aspects of the student's school placements, and although the burden of responsibility of training (and at times it is a burden, though also a professionally rewarding privilege and a pleasure) is very much assumed by the teacher directly responsible for that student, there are clear indications that training students in school should involve a network of others upon whose co-operation depends the quality of the student's training programme.

What is the role of the training institution? The teachers' comments in Section 1 numbered only six. It is not surprising that the items in this category are so few since the teachers were asked only about their own role in relation to the student. Moreover, as subject teachers their links with the UDE are 'personal' – being with the respective methods' tutors – rather than 'institutional'. The formal, institutional link with the UDE is through the professional tutor (deputy head or senior teacher) and therefore for most of the group would not have been applicable. Finally, there may possibly have been a reluctance to express opinions on this relationship since the session was conducted by UDE staff.

If teachers are to be co-trainers of students this means that their complementary training responsibilities must be negotiated and agreed and their unique contribution to training recognised and fully and positively exercised. Drawing up these *Guidelines* for mentors was an early step along this road. This exercise demonstrated the extent to which schools already provide training for students. To have made this explicit and to have used this knowledge as a basis on which to develop more fully the role of the teacher in training was an empowering exercise as the teachers on the course agreed.

## REFERENCE

University of Cambridge Department of Education. (1990). *Guidelines for Mentors and Supervisors*. Cambridge.

*Chapter 3*

# Establishing Criteria
# for Mentoring

Tom Bailey and Mike Brankin

## INTRODUCTION

This chapter describes our introduction to the Licensed Teacher
Scheme during 1990–91 and our approach to it and involvement in it. It
is a personal view based on one year's experience and should not be
taken to imply either that other mentors, schools and licensees should
take the same approach or will achieve the same results. We outline our
feelings and responses to the scheme and make recommendations that
might be used as the basis of a whole-school policy for the training of
licensed teachers. The issues raised highlight aspects of the training that
we consider crucial if the licensee is to have thorough training. In
essence we hope to point the way towards a code of good practice within
school that enables the licensee to teach children successfully while at
the same time also being taught.

In our school there was little knowledge or experience of student
training or indeed knowledge of current teacher training methods. It
was to be starting from scratch. As mentor, I (Mike) have been in
teaching for 13 years and feel up-to-date with current educational
theory regarding Design and Technology, and as head of a large faculty
I have managerial responsibilities and experience.

I, Tom, the licensed teacher, was not without experience of
educational institutions when I first came to the school. After
completing my initial City and Guilds Training in Mechanical Engineer-
ing and working for a number of years in industry, where I was
involved with the training of apprentices, I gained an Open University
BA and Certificate of Education from Bolton Institute of Further
Education. On this course I had gained teaching experience in both
further and secondary education and successfully completed teaching
practices in both. This, however, did not automatically entitle me to

Qualified Teacher Status. The school found out about the Licensed Teacher Scheme in the summer of 1990 and I agreed that this seemed the most appropriate option for me to undertake in order to gain QTS. Mike had been invited by the headteacher to act as mentor and take on the responsibility of steering me through a largely unknown and indeed unwritten course. (It is appreciated that Anglia Polytechnic, which was co-ordinating the scheme locally, had to get it off the ground quickly with very little development time.) Nevertheless, we were determined to be successful from the outset and we were aware that a positive and systematic approach was needed. It was incumbent on both of us, and the school, to devise what we considered to be the most suitable counterbalance to the course that the Polytechnic was offering.

## ON BEING A MENTOR

In retrospect, having taken on this responsibility and experiencing some of the demands made and the skills required, we feel that it is important that mentors are highly qualified personnel with managerial and subject-based experience. They must be committed to the training that they have agreed to undertake. They should have status within the school and good relationships with colleagues as this will enable them to call for and obtain the support and involvement of others throughout the period of training. They need to be familiar with developments in the licensee's subject area and key stages 3 and 4 in the National Curriculum and also up-to-date in their knowledge of different methods of teacher training. They have to be aware of teaching and learning styles and recognise their uses in different contexts. The relationship with the licensee must remain positive and professional as the mentor may have to discipline as well as praise the licensee as the situation demands. Care must be taken to avoid undermining the authority of the licensee by taking over responsibility for decision-making, since the ultimate aim is to foster the licensee's development as an independent and reflective professional.

Perhaps consideration should be given to providing some stringent guidelines in the selection or appointment of mentors. Some form of system for vetting prospective mentors against statutory criteria could be made available to schools. If a mentor had to meet these criteria it would give the role status within the school management structure.

It may not be possible for the mentor to be of the same subject speciality as the licensee quite simply because at the moment licensed teachers are brought in to remedy shortages in staffing. This is not an ideal situation, though with a negotiated programme specifically tailored to satisfy the licensed teacher's needs and with the whole school committed to the training, the non-subject mentor can, through regular liaison with the head of the trainee's subject area, provide a well-structured and worthwhile training experience.

Mentoring is a very tiring, emotionally draining experience. One passes through phases of frustration, anxiety, pleasure and satisfaction. You are forced to reassess your own style of teaching and place your own shortcomings under a microscope. It is vital that these shortcomings are identified and at least acknowledged, if not eradicated, so that they are not passed on to the licensee. It is not the aim of mentoring to produce a clone of the mentor, and the training programme that is developed must ensure this does not occur.

## DRAWING UP A CONTRACT

On the advice of the Polytechnic we decided from the outset that an informal contract between licensee and mentor should be drawn up jointly. This would outline the commitment of both of us to the scheme and would form the basis on which to work. It would enable each of us to feel secure in the knowledge that we shared an understanding of our respective responsibilities. Should things go wrong during the scheme this contract would also act as a safety net and provide a mechanism for sorting out problems.

It is important to establish with senior management the need for protection of all statutory allocated time and for the value of this to be recognised. This ensures that any concerns that either of us have will be dealt with at a given time and on a regular basis without interruption. We felt it important that the contract contained reference to time and venue, target setting, forward planning and the scheduling of the licensee's workload throughout the school calendar. We agreed to hold a regular, formal, timetabled meeting once a week, records of which would be kept by both parties (nobody else would have access to them). Items for the agenda could be offered by either party and would vary from week to week. Major items covered on a regular basis would be lesson unit planning, classroom management and organisation, approaches to discipline, and lesson evaluation. We would keep within these boundaries and deal with no other business. This we felt was an important point to establish. It is always far too easy for either party to be sidetracked into discussing irrelevant topics. A clean-cut sense of purpose was required. We decided that the schemes of work to be taught would be established by the department or faculty but that lesson preparation, record-keeping and evaluation would be the responsibility of the licensee, with advice from the mentor. Other contracted items were that the mentor would provide appropriate and reasonable support in selecting and completing college assignments. At first this area was a little daunting as I knew I could not personally provide all the background or assess accurately the effort or validity of the work done. However, with the involvement and co-operation of senior management, and careful selection of assignments we felt able to cover most angles.

We agreed that the licensee should keep a diary and a detailed planning file to ensure continuity and progression and to have presentable evidence of this for visiting assessors or guests. We felt it important that as well as the teaching and college aspects of the course, a licensee should contribute and be attributed with something that would be implemented and of value to the development of the department. This would be jointly decided on but would essentially give him the opportunity to exercise his personal skills on a project that would be of benefit to the rest of the team.

Alongside the formal meetings, day-to-day problems were discussed and sorted out within the department during lunchtimes after school and at any available moment. The mentor should understand that the beginning teacher will make strenuous demands on his or her time (particularly if the licensee has had only limited exposure to groups of youngsters) and must accept this. Certainly in the first academic year when the licensee is employed as a teacher with the same responsibilities to the children as every other teacher, including a similar workload, it is unlikely that such demands will be tempered, though the nature of those demands will obviously change during this time.

## THE BASIC TRAINING PROGRAMME: PROVIDING A SURVIVAL PACKAGE

For licensed teachers there is little in the way of slow introduction to the educational institution in which they are to work. At worst it is, 'Here is the school, there is your timetable, we will discuss any problems at the end of the week.' Straightforward everyday procedures such as lining up pupils outside rooms, obtaining order before proceeding to speak, speaking over the general working room noise, the use of the chalkboard or the overhead projector, the use of language, the production of aids and differentiated work material – all these need to be addressed if the licensed teacher is to be presented to the class as a professional from the outset. It was also felt to be important to withhold from pupils the true status of the licensed teacher. They do not need to know and it could only serve to undermine pupils' confidence in their teacher.

If a licensed teacher has not had any previous teaching experience or recent exposure to school life, then initial consideration must be given to a number of areas:

1. to what depth does the licensed teacher understand the curriculum that he or she will be expected to deliver?
2. is the licensed teacher conversant with the rules of the school and with the policy of the school on pastoral care?
3. is the licensed teacher fully aware of his or her administrative and pastoral duties as a form tutor?

Some questions will have been answered before the licensee has been accepted on to the scheme, but in order to satisfy initial reservations and apprehensions, we felt it necessary to develop an 'All-You-Need-To-Know-To-Survive-In-This-Institution' package. This means addressing the licensee's needs and devising ways of meeting them. In this way, the survival package is tailored to the training requirements of the individual licensee. In our case, the licensee's package consisted of up-dating subject knowledge with an extra specialist evening course once a week. To address the question of communication and methods of delivery we organised a series of lesson observations with staff in the faculty who were involved in delivering similar subject content. It was possible to arrange this since it is quite common for staff in the faculty to work closely together. Explaining the pastoral curriculum and its associated systems was the task of the school's pastoral co-ordinator and the deputy in charge of probationary teachers. Attendance at all probationary teachers' meetings and assistance from the assistant head of year with the pastoral administration load were also arranged.

## THE FURTHER TRAINING PROGRAMME: WIDER PROFESSIONAL ISSUES

Since the trainee must become acquainted with aspects of school life and with educational issues that go beyond the teaching of the curriculum, it would be useless to concentrate solely on the 'survival package', since this would not extend the licensee's general professional understanding. Teachers, including licensed teachers, have to be aware of the expectations of pupils, parents and governors. They have to be aware of the many roles that as teachers they have to fulfil. But when trying to put a programme together which will include all of these, it is difficult to decide who is the master. Many pressures come to bear.

First, there are the requirements of the DES for the Licensed Teacher Scheme. Second there are the County Guidelines to be adhered to. Third there is the programme to be covered by the college to which the licensee is attached. Then there is the school with its mentor and in-house experts where guidance on subject knowledge and on the philosophy of the subject should be available. Lastly there are the specific needs of the licensee. These may be very different, since the previous experience of licensees will vary so much. In our case, selecting the topics to be covered was done on a 'need-to-know, we-can-provide' basis.

The Senior Management Team (SMT), co-ordinated by the mentor, contributed to the delivery of these topics. Such non-curricular matters as special needs, pastoral care, assessment co-ordination, records of achievement, an understanding of initiatives such as TVEI and LMS – who better to discuss them with the licensed teacher than the senior teachers responsible for these areas in the school? They have the specific facts regarding the institution at their disposal as well as knowledge of the national and regional requirements. They also have direct and often personal access to more specialist information and to county advisory staff if they are needed. Some of the inputs from our SMT were more detailed than others but as tutoring was done in-house, those areas that were inadequately covered could be further researched and an on-going debate could take place.

Since so many of them were involved in the training programme (as having expertise in particular fields), the staff of the school became more prepared to accept lesson observations and to provide school-led INSET as part of normal school procedure, whether the topic was teacher appraisal, equal opportunities, teaching and learning styles, or cross-curricular team teaching. Barriers between subject areas in schools are breaking down and the Licensed Teacher Scheme assists with this process. To supplement this part of the programme, it was arranged that Tom should visit local primary schools. These, and visits to industrial training and post-16 educational establishments would place a secondary school in context and present a licensee with a comprehensive view of the educational system.

## RELATIONSHIPS WITH THE COLLEGE

The relationship between the training institution and the school is crucial and should be carefully nurtured. Areas of responsibility need to be identified and clearly defined so that both sides know exactly what is expected of each other and so that the total training programme is coherent for the licensee. As we were the first cohort through the scheme, planning and preparation time had been minimal and understandably the approach of the Polytechnic was to use units from others courses and adapt them to fit. This was not wholly successful, however. We found that the expectations regarding personal study were unrealistic. The training institution must take account of the workload of teaching preparation, course-work marking and assessment that runs throughout the year. This is a far greater workload than is required of students on traditional PGCE practice. Also assignments must be designed to be relevant for and fully complement work in the classroom. When there are problems in these situations, the mentor will be treated as a shoulder to cry on, and though this role wasn't much relished, the frustration when the lecture programme was not perceived as relevant for the needs of a licensee was appreciated. What really causes the licensed teacher most concern are practical difficulties, such as how to present newly acquired knowledge to unfamiliar groups of children.

But the college programme should not only be about how to teach the licensee's subject. It should also include relevant and necessary background knowledge. All students or trainees following a course leading to the acquisition of QTS should have an understanding of the political pressures that education is subjected to. Courses should address the historical place of education and ensure that students have an understanding of its role in modern society. Psychology and an understanding of the development of children, how they learn and how they socialise are all vitally important ingredients that need careful scheduling in the course in order to get the best response from the licensees. The college link is also an important place to offer trainees the opportunities to come together to share experiences and discuss problems. Many of these will be common and advice and reassurance can be gained from this shared reflection. For a licensee this can be a major aspect of the learning process and one that can only take place out of the school environment.[1]

In conclusion, we must say that as a method of training teachers the Licensed Teacher Scheme has its advantages both for the school involved as well as the licensee. Our school has now gained a fully qualified member of staff who along with a normal teaching load is now leading a team of eight colleagues through a National Curriculum Design and Technology Integrated Project for year 7 pupils.

The danger, however, of opening up this route to teaching more widely may be to have an adverse effect on teacher recruitment in the long term. All sixth form students considering a career in teaching would have the option of following a BEd course or a specialist subject

BA with a mind to joining the Licensed Teacher Scheme later (or doing a PGCE course). If a greater number of students acquire qualifications that could be utilised on the competitive job market outside education, rather than showing a commitment to teaching from the beginning by taking a BEd course, then these students may not find their way into schools and so reduce the number of teachers overall.

## NOTE

1. The course at the Polytechnic is now fully developed and is subject to regular monitoring.

*Chapter 4*

# The Nature and Conditions of Good Mentoring Practice

David Kirkham

## INTRODUCTION

Much of the criticism of teacher training in the past has concentrated on the perceived lack of value of the theoretical studies which used to occupy large parts of the PGCE and BEd courses. A consequence of this criticism is that to a greater extent initial training courses have come to be based in the classroom. But if theoretical studies are relegated to a few essays in an otherwise entirely practical course, or if teaching becomes simply a craft to be picked up in a particular school without reference to research, then the education of pupils will become narrow and inflexible. Good mentoring should be the most direct and fruitful way of showing trainee teachers how the classroom can be theorised and how theory can reflect in turn on classroom practice. This chapter is a consideration of the role of the mentor in linking theory and practice in the classroom and of the conditions under which this might be possible.

It is not uncommon when overseeing a teacher new to the profession to find that there is a cruel difference between educational planning and practice. Schemes that look clear and effective on paper seem suddenly to change under the pressure of events and in the presence of a classroom of children who do not necessarily see themselves as part of the process of teacher training and induction. Were the trainee to refer to theory here, some explanations of these dilemmas might be forthcoming. But he or she cannot always 'feel' the link and when the chips are down, theory tends to get lost. Sometimes it stays lost. This will happen if the trainee decides that the difficulties of early teaching experience are to be solved entirely by a series of hints taken and knacks learnt, particularly if the hints come from more experienced colleagues who have visibly and audibly settled for limited survival strategies in which theory plays little part.

The task of the traditional supervisor is unclear when the student is in this sort of difficulty. The supervisor of a student on teaching practice is often the one who assesses the student's practical ability in the classroom on behalf of the training institution, but otherwise has an ambiguous relationship with him or her. The extent of the supervisor's responsibility for teaching the student how to teach is left unclear, as is the importance which the student should attach to the supervisor's advice. The supervisor usually does not know enough about the detail of the student's course at the training institution and cannot therefore always fit advice to the context, or help in relating theory to classroom events or vice versa. A mentoring scheme gives much greater responsibility for training to the school and to the individual teacher (the mentor).

## GOOD MENTORING PRACTICE IS RELATING THEORY AND PRACTICE

If training is to be based in school, then that training is shared between the university and the school, and the school must have the authority to teach the student. The mentor as envisaged in this chapter is someone who will teach the student and not merely oversee or give advice. Training the student in the school must mean more than giving the sort of sporadic tips that were characteristic of supervision. It must mean systematic support of the student on the long road of professional development, and this means helping the student to see the links between theory and practice, since only if this is accomplished will the student be able to establish the principles of practice or 'rules of teaching' which will enable children to learn.

Mentoring introduces a new and close long-term relationship between trainee and mentor that allows critical concentration on the task involved in teaching. The mentor does not simply instruct the trainee. Teaching is far too much a matter for individual perception and personality for that. The task for both mentor and trainee is to refer to what we know about pedagogy, epistemology and the psychology of learning in order to improve our teaching of particular classes in particular circumstances. It is common for would-be teachers at interview to talk of the pleasure that they derive from their subject and the wish they have to awaken a similar pleasure in others. Everyone would agree that this is an excellent thing and few would disagree with the view that it is essential for successful teaching over the length of a career. It is not enough, however, to see the task solely in these personal terms. Many children do not find the same level of reward in a given subject as that experienced by a specialist who has taken the study to a high level. Under the guidance of a mentor, aspiring teachers would be left in no doubt that teaching is a practical art and skill informed by theory from a number of domains and informing these in turn.

Student teachers know that they should suit their materials, approaches and methods to the age group that they are teaching. But under present teaching-practice arrangements this is usually only done well towards the end of a term, shortly before the student disappears from the school. The student tries things out to see if they work. The supervisor advises, assists and sometimes forbids. But with the help of a mentor, the student could make a systematic attempt to match the structure and coherence of the subject matter to the cognitive and affective development of a particular group of children in a specific context. The art and science of good teaching would come together, as it were.

With good mentoring, the trainee would learn to refer to theory for insights about a particular situation both in planning and in examining the consequences afterwards. Theory is used in a completely practical way. Lessons could be scrutinised and redesigned on the basis of theoretical propositions and of reading until they cease to be experiments in *teaching* (seen largely from the perspective of the student teacher) and become experiments in bringing about *learning*.

This is not to turn the classroom into a laboratory (although in a sense that is what it permanently is). It is to suggest to the trainee that intuition can be informed and may sometimes prove erroneous; that teaching is not merely a matter of applying one's own methods and approaches to a common task, but often a matter of altering and even denying one's own perceptions and intuitions in the light of greater knowledge about what happens when teachers teach and children learn. It is generally accepted for instance that children learn some kinds of knowledge more readily and more reliably when they are given the freedom to pursue an enquiry within a framework designed by the teacher. How is the trainee to be helped to work this way if his or her intuitions and professional insecurities suggest that the best way of teaching is to fold the knowledge up into a bundle and give it to the children by chalk and talk? Support during a probationary year under present arrangements might help him or her to change approaches, and a teacher might also work out independently how to do it, but good mentoring would help to ensure it.

Once teaching is under way, the trainee should always be aware of the declared purpose of each activity or each stage of the course so that he or she may plan for it in conjunction with the mentor. This declared purpose would always be less than the full outcome: it would be the part that is susceptible to planning and forethought. All the rest of teaching is something to be learned only by experiencing it. But good mentoring would at least offer the chance of considering the whole experience, carefully and systematically as it occurs for it would include a full review and account of these events. This should be clearly explained in the description of the course so that the would-be teacher is left in no doubt that teaching consists of more than can ever be contained in a training course, let alone in its prospectus. Mentoring could be the best means yet devised for weaning teachers away from too much dependence on their own learning experiences in school, and for developing in them a readiness to examine their practice and assumptions more effectively. The task of the mentor is to encourage, stimulate, even provoke the student into searching for the principles that will help to ensure that systematic pupil learning takes place. An Articled Teacher Scheme, properly mentored with a well-designed programme in the training institution, could finally bridge the gap between theory and practice. It should assist true child-centred teaching because it could first examine what children need in a general way in the training institution, then what particular children need in a certain time and place, and finally devise a scheme to bring all this together.

This conception of mentoring would not deny the trainee his or her natural style of dealing with children, but it would ensure, as far as is possible, that pedagogy could be developed by the trainee in the light of the best knowledge available. The trainee would no longer be so alone once the theory class is over. It would not be a question of seeing whether something works, but of considering whether it would be the right thing for children generally, why it should work, and how it could be made to work for a class whose needs and reactions are familiar to both trainee and mentor. Learning aims could become more completely the focus of preparation and practice, and if the children do not learn, or learn something unforeseen, the reasons could be sought in a programme of self-assessment undertaken by the trainee with the mentor's help.

## THE CONDITIONS OF GOOD MENTORING

There are at least two conditions of good mentoring as described above. The first is: *that the mentor participates fully in the planning of the student's training*. This is for two reasons. As a teacher the mentor must appear authoritative to the trainee. The mentor must have credibility in the role, and for this to be the case must be well-informed and perceived by the student to be so. It is only if the mentor is fully aware of the details of the course that the trainee is following in the training institution that acting with authority and confidence becomes possible.

Secondly, if the mentor is not aware of what theory is introduced in the university department or college (whether this is the theory of teaching a subject or psychological theory) then how is the student on teaching practice to be helped to use this theory in order to develop a richer and more stable understanding of the events in the classroom? If the student is to receive a coherent and systematic training, in which professional skills and understanding are to develop not on an *ad hoc* basis but in a justifiable and rational manner, then the best and fairest way of achieving this is for the school and the training institution to plan the training course together. For the mentor to be an effective teacher of the student the curriculum of the student's training in school has to be carefully planned and must complement and build on the training provided by the university. The mentor should at least have a hand in shaping the course at the training institution, should know it intimately and should be able to devise a practical course in the school that will enable the trainee to put these ideas into practice without damaging the education of the children concerned.

Time must be found for the mentor to help plan the training course with the tutors. Rushing to meetings after school hours while still trying to do a full-time teaching job is not sufficient. Nor is it sufficient to buy in the mentor's time by paying supply teachers to take some of his or her lessons. This is unfair to the children involved and unfair to the mentor, who is still responsible for the children's progress, even when they are being taught by a supply teacher. This point was well made in a report (by Fran Abrams in the *Times Educational Supplement*, 21 June 1991) on the first year of the government's Articled Teacher Scheme. In the report Alan Smithers of Manchester University spoke of the experience of a consortium that included his university and Manchester Polytechnic: 'We have run it this year on the personal involvement of the staff concerned. They cannot continue doing that.'

The planning team must produce a course that will make clear to the student what is expected and what will be provided. There is no course that could fully prepare a trainee for the complexity of life as a teacher. What can be done is to decide on those aspects of the job that are centrally important, and to work out a way of helping the trainee realise them in theory and practice. (Perhaps the first aspect is to insist to the trainee that the course is initial teacher training, not teaching training. It is only a start.)

The purpose of the course should be declared, as well as its content and its methods, as far as it is possible to specify these, and (by omission at least) those activities, ideas and experiences, that it must leave to daily classroom experience to provide. By concentrating on what can certainly be provided, it can build a framework of understanding within which the unexpected or the unforeseeable may be discussed and understood. It cannot aim to tell a trainee how to copy an experienced teacher's way of organising and controlling a class, but it can concentrate on those considerations which, when fully absorbed, are essential to the successful teacher. And it can then concentrate on the progressive development of these ideas and procedures in practice. We have to adopt Aristotle's idea of expecting from a human activity only such exactitude as the activity is capable of giving. Some parts of whatever is needed to be a good teacher can be specified and taught. Other parts cannot be reached in this way.

The stages of the course, term by term, should be agreed and made explicit, together with the expectations about the trainee's developing involvement and performance. These would be the same in all the schools involved. There should be a description of the relationship of the mentor to the trainee, and the extent of his or her responsibility for the trainee, including the ways in which this should alter during the course with the progressive assumption of a greater teaching commitment by the trainee. These matters might be succinctly expressed in a statement about the trainee's timetable in school. This would include the time that the mentor and trainee might reserve for meetings at various stages of the course. There should be a timetable of the fixed points in the course, both those in the training institution and in the school. In the school, events the trainee would be expected to undertake such as the regular meetings of mentor and trainee, or the programme of observation across the curriculum should be indicated. The manner of assessment should be agreed, including which aspects of it are formative and which are summative. The trainee's involvement in self-assessment should be clearly described. For the benefit of the training institution, the school should outline the induction programme it has arranged for the student. No one's expectations about the course, the school or the trainee's suitability should ever be disappointed, at the level of information at least. The rest would have to be left to the good sense and professionalism of those involved.

Only if the mentor is as fully informed as this, and feels an equal in terms of responsibility for teaching the student, can good mentoring as outlined above take place. For only then can the mentor work actively with the student to relate theory and practice in order to anchor and extend the student's understanding of the teacher's task, and only then will the student perceive the school and the training institution as complementing each other in order to provide a coherent context in which professional learning can take place.

The second condition of good mentoring practice as outlined above is: *that the mentor should have the support and co-operation of colleagues.* The mentor needs time with the trainee, time for discussion and appraisal, and time to relate theory and practice. To help the trainee to do this there should be opportunities and events made available which will encourage the raising of questions, and the challenging of assumptions. The mentor is dependent on colleagues for these. For example, colleagues will be asked if they may be observed teaching in order that the trainee may get to know about teaching styles and can learn to relate these to what goes on in the classroom in a systematic way. Specialist teachers would have contributions to make that could not all come from a mentor. What the mentor needs is the ability to organise and channel the contributions of colleagues. If training is to take place in the school everyone is involved.

The school should be thoroughly prepared for the advent of the trainee teacher, whose status would be impossible to disguise even if anyone wanted to. The position and function of the trainee should be made known throughout the staffroom. The school should undertake not to go beyond the limits of demands on the trainee that it has declared in the programme but should, within those limits, accept the trainee as a member of the staffroom.

The school must agree to allow time for the mentor to spend with the trainee, planning lessons, applying ideas discovered during the theoretical study and reviewing lessons when they have been taught. The trainee should be entitled to expect a full debriefing after each observation made by the mentor. (The meetings at which these observations are reported on by the mentor should follow set procedures, so that embarrassment about criticism – which may become difficult between people who have known each other a long time – may be more easily dealt with.)

The trainee should be aware from the start of the headings under which assessment in the school is to be made. Where necessary this should be made known by the mentor to any other colleague who is helping in the training process. Since no one teacher can be an expert on all that the trainee has to learn in school, training in the end must be a collaborative activity, and there should be a consistent shared policy on the appraisal of the trainee.

Good training in the school (including good mentoring) can only come about if a school takes a principled decision to organise itself for mentoring. The Senior Management Team would have to decide what would be necessary if their school were to take on teacher training. They would have to explain to their colleagues why the school's total staffing budget should be managed so as to allow a mentor time to work with a trainee. Such a decision would necessarily be seen as part of the professional development of all the staff in the school. It should be part of a culture of support and guidance for all new staff whether they are trainees or already qualified. The mentor might lead this aspect of staff development within the school, but all staff should be encouraged to contribute to it and benefit from it.

Mentors of the sort described here are obviously not in plentiful supply, but without good mentors, the whole school-based training programme would be in danger. It would be easy to sympathise with the trainee whose mentor was not given enough time to do the job properly. The trainee would certainly feel dissatisfied and short-changed. The mentor's morale would similarly be poor. Since there is unlikely to be adequate financial provision for Articled Teacher Schemes, part of the saving made by a school that accepts an articled teacher rather than a fully qualified teacher should be compulsorily devoted to buying the time needed for training. This would make the idea less attractive to those charged with guarding the school's budget but the arguments for it are very powerful. Also unpopular would be the need to reward the mentor properly for what is an extremely demanding task. Only experienced teachers should be appointed mentors – people likely to have other responsibilities already apart from their own classes. They need and deserve to be rewarded.

The above principles of mentoring apply equally in an Articled Teacher Scheme or in more traditional forms of training where much of the student's training time is spent in school.

Chapter 5

# Assessment and the Licensed Teacher

Susan Holmes

## THE CHALLENGE OF MENTORING A LICENSED TEACHER

One thing that licensed teachers have in common is that they have little in common! They come from a variety of backgrounds and have very different life histories. Although they must all have attained a certain minimum educational level, their further training needs will differ. For example, a person who had undertaken an overseas ITT course broadly similar in quality and structure to those in the UK might require little further training. Alternatively, a UK graduate with industrial but no teaching experience would need more extensive training. This variability has been noted by H.M. Inspectorate in *Standards in Education, 1989–1990* (1991):

> a broad range of teachers is being recruited under the licensed teacher scheme [LTS] . . . licensed teachers are not a homogeneous group substantially co-ordinated by an LEA: rather they are recruited directly by schools to [fill] specific vacancies and their training needs vary widely. (para 131)

But if licensed teachers have a variable starting point, they also must have a single destination. They must all attain a common standard as practising teachers just as is the case for students on a PGCE or BEd course. Those who are responsible for their training have to make sure that in order to gain Qualified Teacher Status (QTS) licensees should be able to 'demonstrate the necessary personal qualities, subject knowledge and classroom and other professional competence necessary to perform satisfactorily as a beginning teacher'. (Quoted from DES *Circular* 18/89 para 26.)

Since the training of licensed teachers is principally the responsibility of the school then it is the school which has to face and deal with this challenging situation. But the school is a closed institution, complete in itself as an organisational unit, and there may be few opportunities for a mentor to associate with colleagues from other schools in order to establish any notion of a shared standard. The LTS which has been devised by Northamptonshire is designed to meet these difficulties while providing a quality training for its licensees. At its heart are three crucial principles of training (procedures to be adopted). These have a rational basis. They resolve the problem of mediating between the initial uniqueness of outlook and experience that the licensee brings to training and the final goal of a common standard of competency. They are therefore also conditions of good training.

These three principles or conditions are:

- that a 'dialogue of needs' should be established with the licensee;
- that the training (and assessment) programme should be flexible;
- that the judgements of qualified colleagues outside the school must contribute to assessment.

In the following discussion, the way in which these three principles run like threads through the Northamptonshire scheme and how they confront the conflicting demands posed by the individualism of the licensee and the universal demands of QTS will be demonstrated.

## THE NORTHAMPTONSHIRE LICENSED TEACHER SCHEME

It is impossible to separate 'training' and 'assessment'. If assessment or appraisal is to have any meaning or value for the licensee as an indication of the level of his or her achievement, then it must be closely related to the substance of the training that is being undertaken. If it is to have any diagnostic value for the mentor, it must also reflect the nature of the training programme. So a discussion of assessment must also make reference to the training that it reflects.

The Northamptonshire Scheme identifies a number of stages in the training and assessment of the licensee. These are:

1. the Training Assessment Conference;
2. the Training Statement;
3. the Training Record or Portfolio;
4. the Provision of Regular Feedback and Support;
5. termly reporting to the LEA;
6. the Final Assessment Conference.

In addition, it is made clear that assessment is to be a co-operative activity to which the mentor, the professional tutor, the head teacher and an LEA adviser all contribute.

We shall now see how this scheme incorporates the three conditions and so helps to meet the problems mentioned above.

During the first month of preliminary training some estimate will be made of the strengths and weaknesses of the licensee in a number of areas: knowledge of the National Curriculum; subject knowledge; delivery of subject matter; classroom management; teaching styles, strategies and evaluation; the assessment of pupils; and the education system. Following this, the Training Assessment Conference takes place. This is attended by the mentor and the professional tutor in the school, both of whom are by now well known to the licensee and have become aware of many of the trainee's strengths and weaknesses as an intending teacher, and also by a member of the LEA Inspectorate. The purpose of the meeting is to draw up a detailed programme of training for the licensee, taking his or her personal qualities into account. Assessment of the licensee is diagnostic and takes place before formal training begins. The training programme will be based on the licensee's needs in the areas (above) as indicated during the first month. They will be met through a combination of school-based elements, visits to other schools and attendance at training sessions organised through institutions of higher education. Northamptonshire provides mentors and professional tutors with training in drawing up this statement for the licensee. These training sessions provide an opportunity for mentors to share experiences and problems, to organise an exchange of school visits for licensees and to plan the way in which they might use the advisory services.

The outcome of this conference will be a formal Training Statement. This focuses on what will be the responsibility of the mentor for the individual licensee in a number of areas. These include: drawing up schemes of work, the teaching of classroom management skills, the practice of different teaching styles, the focus of visits to other schools, the aims of observation in other departments in the school and special needs and pastoral work (where the head of division makes recommendations for training as necessary). In addition, plans will be made for the licensee to attend the modern languages methodology course run by the LEA advisory team, to attend the course on wider educational issues organised by this team in conjunction with Leicester University and also to attend the probationers' induction programme and their in-service training days. Regular meetings with the licensee are arranged. Also an observation schedule is drawn up which has to be agreed with colleagues. All of this is planned with the particular licensee in mind. The major emphasis of the programme is on training at classroom level.

This was of some concern to my licensee, who felt the need for an extended methodology course such as is the central feature of the PGCE.

Responsibility for devising the way in which the given areas of training are to be interpreted for any individual licensee therefore rests largely with the mentor and the professional tutor, and the mentor is responsible for the implementation of this training programme. The means of training will be much the same for all licensees, but their perceived individual needs will determine how their participation in these events and activities is planned and organised.

The Training Record is the licensee's 'diary' of training. In it are recorded details of the training that has been undertaken, what skills and techniques are being developed and how, what meetings have taken place and what was the focus of these meetings and so on. Also any problems that have arisen and any causes for concern. It will also include the licensee's own personal reflective comments. The Record is a valuable resource at the weekly meetings. It is a focus for discussion. It helps the licensee to recall and convey to the mentor his or her views on progress made, successes (and why these lessons were successful), the need for more guidance in a particular area, and so on.

The Training Record facilitates the flexibility of training. In their joint review of the licensee's comments in it at their meetings, the mentor and the licensed teacher can discuss the need for any adjustments to the training programme.

Frequently the meetings (The Provision of Regular Feedback) with the licensee take the same form. The lesson which has been observed is analysed and for this discussion reference is made to the record of points noted down by the mentor during the lesson. Ways in which improvements might be introduced are then discussed and a plan for the next observation lesson drawn up. It is important to negotiate agreement on what will be the focus of attention on that occasion. These planning discussions will cover the subject matter of the lesson, the ways in which this will be presented and also what is to be expected of the members of the class. What will be their contribution and how do they need to be organised? The lesson plan should allow the licensee to demonstrate not only the specific skills which are of immediate interest and the focus of both practice and analysis with the mentor, but a range of other skills as well. This broadening of the licensee's repertoire of skills is particularly desirable as the training proceeds, since to qualify as a teacher she or he will have to be able to demonstrate a range of competences.

Observation of the licensee and the follow up discussion afterwards have a dual assessment function. Clearly this part of the training procedure is diagnostic and will suggest ways in which the licensee has improved as well as areas in which there is still a need for more practice or for focused instruction. But it is also diagnostic for the mentor. Where it is so important to match the needs of the individual trainee and the programme of training and still bear in mind the distant goal of QTS, any stumbles in the progress of the licensee may indicate that the mentor should reflect on the licensee's capabilities in the context of the demands being made. Did I assess her or his needs here appropriately? Should I not have suggested further practice in this, that she or he try to do it another way? and so on. Ultimately of course, observation of the licensee is to help the mentor to appraise and evaluate for the purposes of granting QTS. Thus it contributes to summative assessment.

In reviewing the licensee's progress since the last meeting, the mentor should not be judgemental but should allow issues to be identified which require further action. The licensed teacher needs to assume ownership of these action proposals, and this can be encouraged by framing them in her or his own personal language. Using the licensee's own phrases and words is a facilitative approach which promotes self-direction and so encourages the growth of confidence.

## THE INCREASING SOPHISTICATION OF TRAINING AND LEARNING

The Training Assessment Conference had produced the first term's programme. At the end of each term, training for the following term is planned. This is done through consultation between the mentor, the professional tutor and the licensee. The headteacher may also attend this meeting. The licensed teacher is asked about her or his needs, and there are also the needs of the mentor to be considered. In both cases, the question is: what further training and support is required?

An important aim now is to extend the experience of the licensed teacher. Observation continues in the school, but opportunities to observe a wider range of teaching styles and methods are made possible through visits to other schools, including local primary schools. The licensee will now be involved in working with GCSE examination pupils and for this careful preparation will be necessary, and support will have to be arranged if required. The requirement that the mentor balance the needs of the individual against the demands of qualification continues. The flexibility of the programme permits this, as the following two examples – concerning a woman trainee – will demonstrate.

By term three of the programme it was felt that sufficient visits to

own initiative or that of the LEA, a school might employ licensed teachers who receive school-based training through the mediation of a mentor. Less formally, schools may assign 'mentors' or more experienced colleagues to ease the induction of teachers new to the school or to the area. Team leaders such as heads of department, year or house would also be responsible for the induction and training of the members of their respective teams. Many schools have systems whereby each person who works in the school has regular meetings for support and supervision with their line manager who undertakes many of the roles ascribed to the mentor. Finally it is quite common for a new headteacher to be assigned a mentor from the rank of experienced colleagues who work in the Authority. It is not unknown for new inspectors and advisers to be given a mentor when first undertaking those roles. Most teachers will therefore be a mentor or have a mentor at different times throughout their career.

## The importance of communication

In the future, teacher training seems increasingly likely to be placed in schools. This makes the need for a consistent whole-school approach to mentor training absolutely essential. Everyone in the school community from the headteacher downwards needs to know and understand the philosophy behind mentoring, the requirement of the mentoring role and those of the various categories of trainee. Regrettably, under the current system this does not always happen in all schools. If training and information are restricted to the two parties who are directly involved (ie the mentor and the trainee), difficulties may arise because other members of the school community may not fully understand the nature of the relationship. These difficulties can be acute when senior staff are not either involved or informed and the necessary time and cover for carrying out observation, discussion, planning and feedback are not forthcoming. A trainee visiting another department or observing the pastoral role of the school can encounter misunderstandings from colleagues if teams are not properly informed about the exact nature of the training being undertaken.

A school culture which places a high emphasis on continuous teacher training enables consistent practice in all departments, and allows effective communication to take place. This can be achieved by drawing up whole-school policies on all aspects of teacher training, articulating the differing needs of each group of trainees, negotiating clear job descriptions and by placing training issues firmly among the priorities identified in the school development plan. If all these processes are carried out with full consultation and debate, staff awareness of training issues and whole-school expectations are enhanced. Trainees in any area of the school therefore should receive the same high level of reflective training to which they are entitled. It will improve the quality of their lessons and directly benefit pupils. The fear that some teachers have of handing over classes to inexperienced teachers should be allayed.

## A common policy on teaching

The definitions of a good teacher are legion, ranging from the narrow instrumental view described in the Teachers Pay and Conditions documents through the behaviourist list of competences used in teacher assessments in other countries such as the USA. Some academics attempt to define broad areas or domains as opposed to checklists of competences, even in some cases prescribing the level of excellence to which trainees should progress at the various stages in their career.[1]

The fact is that there is no one model which can adequately describe effective teaching and be applicable to all teaching situations. While there may be a core of skills and knowledge which are essential for all good teachers to know, such as the structure of the National Curriculum and the ability to keep most of the pupils on task for most of the time, the broad outline of skills and knowledge will differ from phase to phase, school to school and subject to subject. It is essential therefore that each school should debate what it considers to be the main ingredients of effective teaching. The debate should take place in staff meetings, on training days, in team meetings and should result in whole-school and department policies which clearly set out for all comers to the school as well as for existing staff, the expectation of what all teachers in each subject are expected to know and to do in order to give pupils the maximum entitlement. These expectations will be articulated in pro forma for lesson observation, in schemes of work, in agendas for department and task group meetings and in department handbooks and checklists. They will be expressed either in detailed checklists of criteria for performance or in clearly defined broad performance areas or domains. They will be used by mentors for setting expectations to trainees, assessing their progress and setting targets for development, training and improvement. The resulting 'reflection on action' by both trainee and mentor will not only directly affect the pupils whom they teach during the training period, but should mean better classroom practice by new teachers trained in this way.

# WHAT SKILLS ARE NEEDED FOR MENTORING?

## Subject- or phase-specific skills

Our discussion will focus on 'generic' mentoring skills, the core skills which all mentors in education need to develop. It is necessary to stress that these 'generic' or transferable skills are not sufficient on their own to guarantee effective teacher training. There are also phase issues and subject-specific issues which are perhaps even more important for the trainee to acquire. The trainee primary teacher needs to have access to a variety of ways of managing the learning environment. She or he will need to be familiar with the whole curriculum as well as all National Curriculum programmes of study and assessment techniques in Key Stages 1 and 2 as well as progression issues to Key Stage 3. The secondary school trainee will learn the classroom craft in an entirely subject-specific way and will need a detailed knowledge of the National Curriculum framework for that subject as well as having subject expertise at graduate or equivalent level. In addition the trainee will have to learn how to construct programmes of work in a spiral syllabus through Key Stages 3 and 4 which enable children of all abilities and must acquire a thorough corpus of knowledge about resources, methodology, assessment, progression issues, GCSE requirements and so on. All this will be in addition to important whole-school issues, classroom management and organisation, plus pastoral matters.

## Working with partners

The mentor must be able to transmit this subject or phase expertise to the trainee and be able to judge his or her progress at each stage in the training cycle. But it would be unreasonable to expect the hard-pressed individual subject mentor in a given school to tackle the full role of the teacher trainer without any outside assistance. The best way to tackle these specific issues is to work in partnership either with other schools, with institutions of higher education, or with LEA personnel such as advisers or advisory teachers. In this way the mentors have the benefit of peer group support from and discussion with mentors in other schools as well as the theoretical and research input into curriculum matters which acts as a catalyst to developments and innovations in school.

## Generic skills

In addition to subject and curriculum expertise and the ability to communicate them to trainees, the mentor needs core skills which are common to all institutions. They should be included in all mentor training and can be offered in a modular format which enables individuals to opt in or out of specific aspects of training according to need or experience. These skills which are basic to the support and supervision of students are: needs analysis; interpersonal skills such as counselling, negotiation and conflict solving, giving positive and negative feedback; observation and assessment skills; setting targets and report writing. Each of these skills is discussed below. Although each skill is the subject of a separate section it will be clear to the reader that they are in fact interrelated. The success of the mentor in each skill area depends on the extent to which he or she can draw upon the other skills.

## Needs analysis

In order to plan a useful programme of school-based training and development for the trainee the mentor needs to identify the starting point. Knowing about the trainee's previous educational experience enables the mentor to locate the gaps in knowledge which need to be bridged and understand what assumptions the trainee is making about his or her new role. This is particularly important when the trainee has been educated and/or trained in a different sort of school, another part of the country or of the world. If the framework for teaching has already been agreed by the whole school as described above, the mentor can use this to identify what the trainee does or does not know. It also forms a basis for setting expectations and targets.

The mentor also needs to establish what has already been covered in the student's college training (which may have taken place previously or be happening concurrently with the period of mentoring) so that he or she can best establish the relationship between theory and practice. Probationary teachers have been known to lament that they are obliged to attend induction sessions which only repeat what they have already learnt at college and do not advance their expertise. This would be easy to avoid if a survey of training needs were carried out by the mentor at the start of each stage in the training cycle.

The development of needs analysis skills in teachers will help them to plan individual learning programmes for pupils, provide differentiated work for pupils of different abilities and offer appropriate guidance when pupils are making subject, course or career choices.

## Counselling

The skills associated with counselling are imperative to successful mentoring. There are various models, one of the most common being the Egan approach to effective helping.[2] This model describes stages of counselling as:

1. identifying and clarifying problem situations and unused opportunities;
2. goal setting – developing a more desirable scenario;
3. action – moving toward the preferred scenario.

Integral to the process is the concept of 'client self-responsibility' which is strengthened by success, modelling, encouragement and reducing fear or anxiety. The relationship between these skills and the need for the mentor to enable the trainee teacher to reflect on his or her own practice, and thus progress in a developmental fashion, is self-evident.

Teacher training is essentially about the classroom craft, articulating the knowledge, theory, skills and experience which make trainees into good teachers. Traditionally, the theoretical aspects of pedagogy have been the remit of HE institutions. Teachers have not necessarily shared in the process of defining explicitly the ingredients of effective teaching or developing the concept of the 'reflective practitioner'. Teachers who teach well do so intuitively. The craft is implicit rather than explicit and we cannot assume that the best teachers are automatically equipped to pass on their expertise to others. They may need to be trained to do so. The mentor needs to be able to reflect upon and define this craft for him- or herself if the trainee is to be enabled to do likewise. Successful counselling by the mentor will both depend on and enhance the ability of the trainee to be self-aware and engage in constructive self-appraisal of his or her practice.

Effective teachers will use counselling skills to enhance the achievements of children. This applies not only to the teacher's disciplinary or pastoral role (to solve conflict or enable pupils to work through difficult circumstances at home or at school) but also to the academic role. The three steps described above can be used when giving pupils guidance and support in working out their own action plans, either in individual subjects or when moving through transitional phases, for example between Key Stages or between secondary and tertiary education or into the world of work. They are also of use when preparing pupils to write their statements for records of achievements.

### Negotiation and conflict solving

The mentor needs to negotiate with the trainee and with other colleagues who are helping (or hindering) in the training process: college staff, senior management, teachers in other schools and other departments, or even the trainee him- or herself. Some of the issues for negotiation can be delicate and there are many opportunities for conflict to arise. For instance, one of the difficulties in the role of the mentor as applied specifically to student or licensed teachers is in the tension which can arise between the mentor's role as 'critical friend' and supporter and that of assessor and examiner. It is not unknown for personality clashes or conflicts between mentor and trainee to occur. Highly developed negotiation skills are therefore necessary and training is essential.

The basic skills of good negotiation are: anticipating and avoiding possible conflict, non-confrontational verbal or body language, good verbal and non-verbal communication, choosing appropriate settings for the negotiation to take place, clearly identifying and separating issues, the ability to review and summarise the other person's points, acknowledging the value of the other person's point of view and identifying issues of agreement.

The negotiator must also remember some key principles which can equally well be applied to counselling and giving feedback. It is important that all parties involved are able to maintain their self esteem at all stages in the negotiation. This can be achieved by making sure that their *views* are acknowledged and valued. Sarcasm, anger and intimidation must be avoided and separate issues should be dealt with as such. Everyone must be equally involved in solving the problem. Mentors can learn to take the following steps when solving a conflict:

- describe the situation and review previous discussions;
- ask for the reasons for the situation;
- listen and respond with empathy;
- indicate what action you must take and why;
- agree on specific action and follow up date;
- indicate your confidence in the parties involved.[3]

Negotiation and problem-solving skills are useful to teachers in sorting out discipline problems between pupils. In this way confrontations can be avoided and disruption to lessons minimised. This increases the amount of time pupils spend on task and thus helps to raise their achievement.

## Giving and receiving positive and negative feedback

Giving positive feedback and praise is easy although we may not do it often enough, whether to pupils or to colleagues at all levels. Most of us balk at giving negative feedback or give it in inappropriate settings like full staff meetings or in front of the whole class. It is very hard to sit down with a colleague and tell him or her about any failings. Many teachers and teacher trainers employ quite ingenious and tortuous strategies to avoid doing so altogether. We may split our sides at the training video which shows the college tutor debriefing the student after a particularly disastrous lesson but this completely avoids the real issues and targets for improvement in a misguided attempt not to demotivate or hurt the feelings of the already struggling trainee.

The hard truth is that as a classroom teacher or a mentor we will never effect any real change in the performance of those for whom we are responsible if we never tell them clearly and unequivocally what it is that they are doing wrong. The quality of the feedback is the single most important factor in this aspect of staff development. There are several basic principles which make this easier.

First, it helps when negative feedback (which is of course a euphemism for criticism) is balanced with some positive feedback (or praise). When debriefing a trainee it is useful to list all the things that went well as well as those that went badly. A balanced view is easier to accept. The trainee receiving the feedback needs to feel that the mentor or supervisor genuinely values them.

Second, it is essential to stick to fact, things which were observable, rather than opinion. A checklist or pro forma to which we have already referred (above) provides a useful framework for this.

Starting the feedback session by asking the trainee for his or her own views on the performance: 'How do you think it went?' usually elicits an honest response and may preclude your having to bring the matter up at all.

The setting and the external circumstances for giving feedback are also crucial. The interview should take place in a private and comfortable room and should be free from interruptions. The use of a positive tone of voice, of body language and of eye contact is also important. Raised voices and pointing fingers should be avoided at all costs.

It may be of course that the mentor is on the receiving end of negative feedback and there are also techniques which serve to defuse potentially difficult situations. For instance, listen carefully without interrupting, always accept the feedback at face value and if at all possible welcome it. Statements like, 'Thank you for those comments, I shall give them my full consideration' are helpful especially if they are meant genuinely. It is not useful to counter-attack. Comments such as, 'That's not fair, your punctuality is even worse than mine!' only cloud the issue under discussion. Nor should you have to justify your position: 'Well, I had to take over your lesson because you were making such a shambles of it.' Equally the person on the receiving end should not become angry or emotional.

It is helpful, when you have received or given the feedback to proceed to 'clarify' or 'explore' the issues – 'O.K. Let's explore the reasons for your difficulties with 9M.' 'I'd like to clarify with you why your lesson

didn't work.' When problems have been identified in this way it is
ample to proceed to targets for improvement and the recipient of the
feedback will feel that the session has been truly developmental rather
than negatively destructive.

These skills have a similar value to those of counselling. They enable
teachers to support individual pupils' academic and pastoral progress
and to defuse confrontation in the classroom. They can also be used in
option choice, careers and guidance interviews.

*Observation and assessment skills*

Observation skills are vital to the mentoring role from various
perspectives. The mentor must help the trainee, particularly if he or she
is undergoing initial training, to learn from the observations and
shadowing he or she carries out of more experienced colleagues,
including the mentor. Before students or articled teachers begin the
gradual easing into classroom teaching they must observe a wide
variety of teachers, styles, age ranges, ability levels, subjects and schools
in all phases. Both mentor and trainee need to clarify the focus and
purpose of these observations and to be able to reflect and draw
conclusions from them. In fact the ability to observe more experienced
teachers or one's peers in order to reflect upon teaching skills is a
prerequisite of the whole-school approach to enhancing classroom
performance in a reflective way. Many institutions use peer observation as an integral part of their staff development programme.
Observation of classroom performance is an integral component in
schoolteacher appraisal and should be used in a problem-solving rather
than a judgemental fashion.

The trainee will also be observed regularly by the mentor and others.
Most of these occasions will be entirely developmental, focusing on
certain skills and measuring progress since the previous observation.
There will also be formal observations which take place for assessment
purposes at key points in the training cycle and which will result in a
written report as well as the usual debriefing.

Whatever the purpose of the observation, it requires careful planning
and negotiation and not all teachers can be assumed to possess
automatically the necessary skills for effective observation. It is
important for school managers to facilitate effective and developmental
use of observation not only by organising training but by making sure
that both mentor and trainee have adequate time to plan, carry out and
assess observations. In this age of innovation overload and dwindling
resources that is not always easy to do.

The two most widely used styles of observation are clinical supervision and partnership or democratic supervision. Supervisors in the first

category follow their own focus for observations, usually according to a pro forma or system widely in use in their institution and which should be known to the trainee. This is the style most frequently used by teacher trainers in HE. Issues to be discussed at the debriefing session are decided by the supervisor and targets are set according to his or her perceptions. Partnership supervision implies that the mentor and trainee agree together the focus for the observation, perhaps arising from the trainee's own concerns and perceived difficulties. The observation, written report, debriefing and subsequent targets are then planned and negotiated jointly. This model is the one which is most suitable for school-based teacher training and for peer observation. It is most conducive to the empowerment of the trainee to develop her or his teaching skills in a reflective mode.

The separate stages for each partnership observation are:

- plan the focus of the observation and establish whether it is developmental or for the purpose of formal assessment;
- agree the time and place for the observation;
- agree how the observer will function during the observation either as a 'fly on the wall' or as a participant in the lesson;
- agree an adequate period of time and a private place for debriefing;
- carry out the observation making a written record;
- give brief informal feedback at the end of the observation, keeping comments as positive as possible;
- debrief formally as soon as possible after the observation, basing feedback on the written script which records factual data according to the agreed focus. It is important to debrief in a setting where interruptions can be avoided and privacy guaranteed;
- agree with the trainee targets to be met and/or the focus for the following observation;
- if the observation is for formal assessment purposes state clearly to the trainee what recommendation you will make following this observation and explain why, based on the factual report and agreed targets.

The focus which is agreed for the observation will differ according to the stage in the training cycle and the trainee's own progress. Logically, at the beginning of the training period the trainee will need more guidance from the mentor when establishing the focus of an observation and discussion will be more general. As the transition to a full teaching timetable proceeds specific items of concern and interest will present themselves naturally either to the student or the mentor. Topics could include: beginnings and endings of lessons; race and gender issues; 'on task' observation of specific pupils of differing abilities; use of resources; class control techniques; questioning techniques; classroom management issues such as seating arrangements and record keeping; use of writing in lessons, etc.

The emphasis of classroom observation lies in improving teacher performance, and this means improved pupil achievement. Observation can be focused on general teaching procedures or on the needs of individual pupils or groups in order to monitor their performance and to set targets for improvement. Inevitably pupil achievement will benefit.

## Report writing

Clearly, written reports on the professional progress of individuals must not be based on subjective opinion which cannot be corroborated in the event of disagreement or grievance. The language used should be neutral and professional. Reports should refer only to fact and not to personal opinions.

When looking at the whole-school approach to teacher training we indicated the need for an agreed set of criteria which represents the school's view of effective classroom teaching. Such criteria of which everyone is aware provide the necessary objective and neutral basis for report writing.

Mentors and supervisors may be required to write reports on a number of occasions. Reports are needed in the interim and final assessment of probationary teachers and the interim and final assessment of students, articled and licensed teachers. Report writing in an objective, structured and professional way is therefore a skill which all mentors need.

The diagnostic use of written reports on pupil progress at the end of a Key Stage, unit or module helps both teacher and pupil to identify weaknesses and set targets for the next stage.

## Setting targets

The aim of teacher education and training should be to enable 'reflection with a view to action' by the individual.[4] In other words to help people to do their job better. Both mentor and trainee need to be able to identify achievable targets for improvement through the process of discussion, observation and evaluation. This latter element can be self-evaluation of performance as well as joint evaluation by both partners in the training process.

Inevitably it is more difficult for the inexperienced teacher to identify targets for improvement in their own performance without some assistance. The framework of criteria or domains described above provides the basis for this process as well as for supervision by the mentor.

The formal structure of the feedback or debriefing with an agenda agreed in advance, aids the process of self-evaluation and setting of targets. The debriefing begins with a review of strengths and weaknesses and culminates with the negotiation of targets. A debriefing of any sort without identification of targets for the next stage is virtually useless. If the trainee knows that the agenda will conclude with the agreement of objectives to be attained by the next debriefing he or she will usually come to the meeting with a set of prepared targets. Should that not be the case the mentor or supervisor will give carefully prepared feedback as described above, both positive and negative, based on observed data and the written record. The targets for improvement will arise naturally from the areas for concern which have been discussed.

The appraisal scheme implemented by the Suffolk Education Authority gives clear guidance on setting targets, which can be adapted to any situation involving mentoring or supervision. 'Targets to improve teaching effectiveness should be specific, realistic, challenging, achievable and commensurate with the resources available. They should be limited in number (3–5), clear on both the teacher's plans for achievement and the intended results.'[5]

The setting of targets for both teachers and pupils to cover a pupil's progress from one level of attainment to the next is crucial to the success of the National Curriculum and to the achievement of individual pupils.

## THE WIDESPREAD BENEFITS OF MENTORING SKILLS

It has been shown above that once a mentor has acquired these skills for use in the mentoring role, they can also be practised in the classroom for the benefit of the pupil. Counselling, negotiation, conflict solving, giving and receiving positive and negative feedback and setting targets are all skills integral to the support and supervision of pupils as well as trainees. They therefore should form part of every teacher's training at some time.

The acquisition and practice of these skills is as important for teachers as managers as it is for them in their classroom role. For example, needs analysis should be the starting point when planning any staff development programme, whatever the level of seniority of the participant. It is as necessary and relevant for an articled or licensed teacher, a probationary teacher or an experienced colleague who is new to the school as it is for the student. Counselling, negotiation, conflict solving, giving and receiving positive or negative feedback and setting targets are all skills integral to the support and supervision of staff as well as students and pupils and should form part of all management training. They can be used in the teacher's pastoral role with both pupils and parents and in the line management of support and teaching staff. Teachers who have undertaken training in these key areas report that their interpersonal skills are greatly enhanced in all aspects of their work as a result. Negotiating and conflict solving skills are particularly important to senior managers, given the wider range of new responsibilities acquired by heads and governors with local management of schools and in grant-maintained schools.

School managers, just as much as classroom teachers, will meet conflicts in their daily work and the ability to resolve these and also to act as a counsellor where necessary can radically improve relationships with staff colleagues, parents or governors. All middle and senior managers in schools have the dual responsibility of supporting and monitoring those in their teams as well as helping team members to evaluate and reflect upon their own practice. Here the systematic use of peer observation can be a valuable and cost-effective means of staff development. The definition of targets is an integral part of any school development plan, but is also a means by which any teacher can be encouraged to raise the quality of his or her teaching. Writing reports in a succinct, professional and objective manner is an important skill for all teachers. Reports are needed for writing papers for senior staff, for describing incidents in school, for minuting appraisal meetings, for matters relating to staff discipline. The skill of report writing is needed in pastoral work for referral to other agencies or in writing to parents, and in the academic role in the compilation of records of achievement. Finally the ability to work in partnership with others is a prerequisite for the effective running of any organisation. Most of us can do this intuitively but when groups or individuals are unable to do so, dysfunctions in the smooth running of the institution may come about and can affect everyone.

Training in these skills can therefore have benefits for the school as a whole and not just for their mentors, their trainees and their pupils. They will help all staff in their management role.

We tend to assume that teacher training only occurs during the brief period when Bachelor of Education (BEd) or Postgraduate Certificate of Education (PGCE) courses are being undertaken by the 'student', or for the duration of the 'licence' period in one of the more recent forms of 'on the job' teacher training. This is not so. Henry Morris, the idealist of the community college movement in Cambridgeshire, articulated the need for a continuous process of teacher training in 1941 in a memorandum to the Association of Directors and Secretaries for Education: 'We have somehow to find a method of ensuring that the education and technical training of teachers goes on throughout their careers . . .'[6] The James Report of 1972 endorsed this view by recommending that the education and training of teachers 'should be seen as falling into three consecutive stages or "cycles": the first, personal education, the second pre-service training and induction, the third inservice education and training.'[7]

The discussion above suggests that mentoring can be seen as a process which contributes not only to the training of the 'trainee' who is likely to be at an early stage in his or her career, but also to that of the mentor, who will be at a later stage in the cycle, when higher-level skills are required. Thus ideally, the training of teachers would take place not only during their period of initial training but as a continuous cycle which to some extent begins with the individual's own educational experience, continues through higher education and teacher training, is developed in the probationary period and/or early years of teaching and continues with inservice training and professional development until the end of the practitioner's career.

# REFERENCES

1. *Times Educational Supplement*. (7.9.90). 'What Makes a Good Teacher?' An article by Suzannah Kirkman describing the 9 dimensions of teaching defined by staff at St Luke's College in Exeter. Each dimension contains 8 levels.
2. Egan, G. (1986). *The Skilled Helper*. Brookes Helm.
3. Development Dimensions International. (1984).
4. Elliot, J. (1979). 'Preparing Teachers for Classroom Accountability', *Education for Teaching*, 100, p. 55.
5. Suffolk Education Department. (1987). *In the Light of Torches. Teacher Appraisal. A Further Study*, p. 22.
6. Ree, H. (1973). *Educator Extraordinary. The Life & Achievements of Henry Morris*, Harlow. Longman.
7. DES. (1972). *Teacher Education & Training* (The James Report), HMSO.

# PART II   Mentor Training

## Chapter 7

# An Experiment in Mentor Training [1]

Chris Watkins

## INTRODUCTION

This is a preliminary account of an experiment in school training mentors. It is clearly a preliminary account since the experiment is still under way. It is also a partial account in that it is mainly composed by the present author. A further collaborative account which is more explicitly based on the views of all the mentors involved is planned and currently being developed. Meanwhile, this paper is mainly descriptive, partly reflective and from the perspective of the 'tutor', with all the limitations this implies. It will mainly focus on the ideas and practices we have addressed. At this stage it is not possible to give a formal assessment of the impact of the experiment. Informal feedback and evaluation has been going on throughout and has been very positive on occasion.

## BACKGROUND

With hindsight it seems important to describe the scheme in which the mentoring and mentor training took place. This is necessary in order to make sense both of the approach and of the issues which were faced during the experiment. The fact that this was mentoring for initial training of teachers (ITT) through the Articled Teacher Scheme (ATS) beginning in 1990 has considerable effect on how similar or different it may be to mentoring in other contexts and in other schemes. This description will therefore start with a brief look at the scheme itself and the history behind the mentor training.

The ATS was a collaborative effort beteween training institutions and Local Education Authorities (LEAs). The very first proposals submitted to the DES made mention of an accredited course of training for mentors. Beyond this there was little detail. In our early planning meetings between the various parties, key decisions were made about the role of the school mentor (professional tutor). In those meetings there was a strong voice from LEA colleagues that mentoring for ITT should be integrated with other staff development processes in the school. As the scheme was directed towards the training of teachers for secondary education this meant that the mentoring should relate as effectively as possible to other staff development processes in the secondary schools. The important implication was that the first target for training and provision would be colleagues in secondary schools who had a whole school, cross-subject brief and who were likely to be members of staff with already existing responsibilities. The scheme was funded in such a way that the costs of providing teaching cover for these colleagues for something approaching 0.1 of the week were to be passed to the schools, and that this time would mainly be used for running small group mentor sessions. There were to be on average three articled teachers per school.

Another historical influence which became increasingly important was the design of the articled teachers' course. Decisions about the aspects which would be addressed in the early stages and the aspects which would be addressed in the institution-based experience have major implications for what is to be addressed and developed in other contexts, especially that of the school. In the very rushed planning a quick decision was made that much of the initial stages of the teacher training would consider content and classroom process issues, with early input focusing on this in the Institute, while the broader orientation to school and the professional issues emanating therefrom would be more fruitfully handled from a school-based starting point. As a result a rather too easy split between subject and professional issues took place. A further influence was the person who had become tutor for mentor training and who wished to give explicit reference to the supervision skills involved in mentoring and to the professional and personal transition which is so important for people entering training for teaching.

As a result of all of these influences a first draft description of the major aspects of the school mentor's role took the shape shown below (Figure 7.1). This role description attempted to identify possible skills to be exercised in the role in order that the agenda for training could be more effectively and explicitly discussed in terms of these same skills.

**Figure 7.1**   *Preliminary role outline*

---

- Who is a school mentor (professional tutor)?
  It is hoped that the mentor in the ATS will be a senior member of staff
  who already has some responsibility for the care and development of
  staff – a staff tutor, a teacher with responsibility for co-ordinating staff
  development, and so on.

- What is the role?
  The role of the school mentor has three major overlapping aspects
  (each expanded below):

  - a. pastoral support to a new teacher
  - b. supervision
  - c. sequential introduction to professional issues in education

Regarding (a) above:
In this aspect the mentor will be aiming to support the personal process of
choosing teaching as a career at the same time as dealing with some of
the many practical problems which can beset someone of any age in
London. Knowledge and understanding of the processes in becoming a
teacher, and the issues which face new teachers will be important. Skills
of helping someone reflect on personal choice and personal difficulties at
a time of change will be needed, together with skills of handling
professional boundaries in this area, and where necessary skills and
knowledge for referring to other sources of help

Regarding (b) above:
In the teaching profession supervision is not what it can be in industry
(overseeing and inspecting), nor what it is in social work (accountability
for statutory casework). It is support and facilitation to enable someone to
become more effective, and is geared to their needs. Skills of supervision
include:

  - developing an appropriate climate and forms of communication;
  - encouraging reflection and review of performance;
  - aiding self-evaluation and identifying needs;
  - giving constructive feedback;
  - supporting enhanced understanding of the other's situation and their
    position in it;
  - problem-identification and support in problem-solving;
  - helping to generate development;
  - helping to set goals and review progress.

It is probably important that supervision in our Articled Teacher Scheme is
likely to take place in the context of a small group. The extra perspectives
available through this arrangement are a great strength to all.

Regarding (c) above:
This aspect recognises the range of professional issues a teacher will
meet, and supports the new teacher's examination of these. It is likely to
be effective if handled in a problem-solving style. It is probably useful to

recognise that there is a plethora of views (CATE, school, LEA, Institute) on what these professional issues should include. Knowledge and understanding of these professional issues and their occurrence and resolution in the particular school will be needed. The following skills will be necessary:

- negotiating a professional agenda;
- using a range of resources for learning;
- supporting school-based investigation; and
- supporting the writing of professional accounts.

## THE EXPERIMENT COMMENCES

### Day One: The scheme and the role of the school mentor

So it was that in 1990 the first meeting of seven senior colleagues from London comprehensive schools took place in which we attempted first of all to understand the Articled Teacher Scheme. We then examined the above draft of the role of the mentor. This draft seemed to be well received. Only then could we move on to discuss what the training for mentors might comprise. We presented the outline of a programme of training which had been developed from the role description (see Figure 7.2)

**Figure 7.2** *Preliminary outline of training*

Before the year starts:
   2 days on the role of mentor, the anticipated needs, and perspectives on becoming a teacher.

At the start of the year:
   1 day in the induction week, to include a session in which mentors and ATs meet in the Institute context.

In Term 1
   2 days on skills of supervision and support.

In Term 2
   1 day on supporting development.

In Term 3
   1 day on assessment of teaching performance.

Through the year:
   'Twilight sessions' on themes such as organising school-based sessions, developing the 'education issues' etc.

In practice the scheme of training did not fit this plan exactly, as the following extracts partly show.

## Day Two: Relations between teachers, tutors and trainee teachers

Writing a role description does not create a role and in the introductory sessions of the ATS we managed to organise an opportunity for some of the main participants to meet. These were the articled teachers, the Institute tutors and the school mentors. During the induction week programme all parties met in the same room, and engaged in some active first introductions. Using an article written by Boydell (1986), and also some ideas from family casework we considered the possible relationships which could exist between the various participants. These included some of the old, almost archetypal stories of teacher training (see Figure 7.3).

**Figure 7.3**  *Notes on 'triangle relations'*

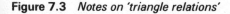

One of the things you may have noted about the Articled Teacher Scheme is that there are quite a number of people involved. Key people are the trainees themselves, their teachers, and the tutors at the Institute of Education. Other people include the coordinating mentors in the schools (often known elsewhere as the professional tutors) advisers in the LEAs and so on.

As a way in, it's useful to remind ourselves of some of the time-honoured stories about teacher training, in particular about:

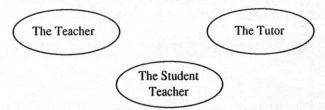

When you put these three together, you may get some interesting dynamics. Here are some of the possibilities:

1.

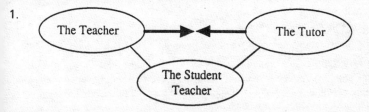

Example 1 portrays a situation in which there is poor communication between the tutor and the teacher. We're doing our best to avoid this, but when it happens all sorts of things can go wrong. It's rather like a family in which each of the 'adults' can end up blaming the 'child' for anything that goes wrong. The teacher or the tutor can fall into the trap of saying to the student teacher *Don't listen to them: listen to me*. Or the student teacher can end up carrying messages of one to the other, in a form of *They said you should*. On other occasions the student teacher may end up in the position of the child who plays one off against the other, or alternatively keeps them both apart rather than suffer because of the poor communication.

2. The next example is one where people in the triangle take sides:

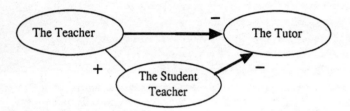

This portrays a game called 'Get the Institute'. It's a situation in which the teacher might be saying to the student *That Institute's an ivory tower – they couldn't teach*, and the student teacher might be saying to the tutor *My supervisor in school is marvellous*. In this way a cozy relation or coalition between student teacher and teacher builds up. But it's not realistic. We should recognise it for the collusion it is.

3. The mirror of the previous example is the game of 'Get the school':

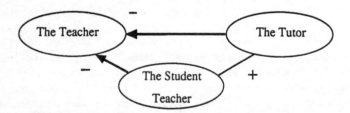

Here the tutor might fall into saying to the student teacher *We're sorry we had to put you in that school*, and the student teacher says to the tutor *They don't help me at the school. I wish the school was more like the Institute*. Again, they're sharing a simple and unrealistic view of the world.

4. The last of the logical possibilities for taking sides in this triangle is one that I don't have experience of. It's 'Get the student':

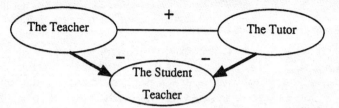

This one would certainly be most unhealthy because it's rather like parents ganging up on the child. But having introduced the idea of unhealthy triangles, that now allows us to be clear about the features of the healthy triangle:

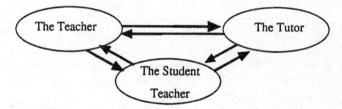

In this situation:

- people are clear about:

  their different roles.
  their different perspectives
  their different learning needs

- they communicate openly and frequently, and they treat each other as adults

---

One of the more surprising aspects of this event was that the articled teachers gathered from a range of countries and cultures, showed clear recognition of the stories which this device allowed us to tell. We ended with a discussion of how to maintain a healthy triangle. This led to exercises in which the three groups of participants identified, exchanged and discussed their learning needs in the new scheme, and identified the ways in which they might fall into the various traps. This gave an important focus to the issue of effective communication between all three parties including the idea that communication between any two should always mention communication between other pairs. At key points, as the scheme has since developed, it has been interesting to note that various people have referred to the notion of triangles in order to communicate something about relationships.

With those features in the background the meetings of mentors with a focus on skills development began.

## Day Three: First focus on supervision skills

Early training sessions which proved important focused on the notion of supervision. Here we were admirably helped by Martin Powell, Principal Educational Psychologist in Birmingham, who had examined the processes of supervision in initial training of educational psychologists.

First we reviewed our own experiences of being supervised, in teaching and elsewhere. The trends were clear:

- few people experienced supervision in their roles as practising teachers;
- most people experienced something which might have been supervision in their initial training as a teacher;
- this was closely allied to evaluation and judgement;
- a few people had experienced detailed supervision of developing skills while on 'long' INSET (ie some years ago before INSET became so fragmented and reductionist).

Our starting definitions of supervision made reference to a number of points (see Figure 7.4).

**Figure 7.4**  *Starting views on what supervision comprises*

- assisting someone to reflect critically
- guiding and supporting
- watching and working
- supporting and building
- leading by example
- winning respect
- helping, guiding, advising, giving praise
- two-way process of responsibility
- standards of performance, and how to attain them
- ability to persuade, gain commitment, inspire
- reviewing progress and looking ahead, setting priorities

The most apposite conclusion to draw was that this was no mean task!

The survey Martin Powell had been involved with offered evidence on what people found difficult:

- trainees report that they are concerned about receiving too little critical appraisal from the supervising teacher, while

- supervisors and tutors report they are concerned about dealing with unsatisfactory work by the trainee, and that this is difficult to tackle.
- trainees and supervisors both find it difficult to deal with the incompatible value system of the other although they don't report this happening often.

An aspect of the skills involved in supervision was addressed in a particular way, using ideas developed from the work of Chris Argyris. This alerts us to:

- in interactions we often choose 'one up–one down' strategies, creating 'win–lose' situations;

**Figure 7.5**  *'Footprints' in supervision conversations*

---

1. Enquiry without advocacy
   in which the reason for asking is not disclosed. For example:

   *Why did you choose that topic?*
   *What were you trying to do when you . . .*

2. Advocacy without enquiry
   making statements which require the other person to do something, but without checking whether they're understanding/able/interested. For example:

   *Read this article*
   *The school handbook says you should . . .*

3. Unillustrated attribution and evaluation
   which show that you've reached conclusions but don't disclose why. For example:

   *I thought that was a successful lesson. What did you think?*
   *Well that's all you should expect from a Year 9 class.*

4. Undisclosed and privately tested assumptions
   these don't let the other person know what you are really getting at. For example:

   *How is your record of observations going?*
   (while privately thinking the person hasn't done one).
   *I think you should work with a tutor group*
   (while wondering how the person will react to your suggestion).

5. Unfocused advocacy
   not establishing, maintaining or checking out a common topic. For example:

   *We need to talk about school policies today.*
   *One of the most important skills of the teacher is to clarify objectives.*

---

- we focus on ourselves and pursue our own goals;
- we take and keep control in interactions;
- we protect ourselves, so we don't 'let on' when we're confused;
- we assume that being effective is being powerful;
- we avoid generating negative feelings in ourselves/in others.

Argyris terms these 'governing values', and contrasts a control model (as above) with a democratic model. This device allowed us to see the trap of handling supervision in a controlling rather than a democratic manner. Governing values in turn give rise to 'theories of action' which, rather like grammar in language, we use without reflection. Examining these further encouraged us to analyse evidence of the control exercised in everyday conversations. These can be termed the 'footprints' of conversations (see Figure 7.5).

Although the phrases were at first unfamiliar, the ideas seemed to have impact. It became possible to identify such 'footprints' in spoken interchanges and also in written communications. It also became possible to think about conversations which contained fewer 'footprints', for example:

- *I feel we'll use this time most profitably if we take a few minutes to decide what we want to discuss and what we want to get out of it. Do you agree?*
- *I would find it valuable, and I'd be less likely to misinterpret, if you first told me about (for example, your goals). Would that cause any difficulty?*
- *There are a number of things we could talk about – we've talked a lot about classrooms – do you have a view on what we should focus on?*

The device of 'footprints' helped us to derive some of the key principles in holding conversations of a supportive nature (see Figure 7.6).

**Figure 7.6**   *Key principles in supervisory conversations*

---

- negotiate your role explicitly, taking care over the evaluative dimension;
- ask the teacher what he/she wants you to report on and discuss;
- if you ask questions, give your rationale for asking;
- don't make judgements without clarifying their basis, in detail;
- beware of regarding the discussion as an opportunity to control.

---

A further stage in the development of skills gave explicit attention to the ways in which supervisors may bring the notion of change into their conversations. Sometimes this is not a problem, but sometimes the notion of change is avoided, never quite addressed. The theme was investigated in two stages:

**Stage One**   considered how conversations can get the theme of change onto the agenda. Conversations about particular aspects of becoming a teacher which include:

- *What would you like to be different?*
- *How would you like things to be in the future?*

can develop an idea of the learner's overall goal.

Conversations which include:

- *What can you do to effect this?*
- *What steps can you take first?*
- *Who can help?*
- *Who else needs to be involved?*

can start to address the practicalities of change.

Useful questions that the supervisor could encourage the student to ask themselves might be:

- *What would this (problem situation) be like if I were to feel more competent?*
- *What would I be doing that was different?*
- *What would be happening which isn't now?*
- *What would I not be doing?*
- *What would I have that I don't have now?*
- *What would other people be doing that they aren't now?*

**Stage Two** addressed the practicalities of how someone might think about and support change in their developing personal and professional repertoire (see Figure 7.7).

**Figure 7.7** *Principles when helping someone to make a change*

---

- work from the learner's motivation so that the change helps them achieve something they want, helps them feel more competent;
- adopt an approach which stresses experimentation and learning, rather than appearing to say that there's a single 'right answer' out there to be discovered;
- anticipate and discuss what will constrain change and what will promote it;
- pick up and examine strategies from other sources credible to the student, models they choose. Do not fall into the trap of thinking that you've got to come up with the ideas, or that your ideas will prove credible to them;
- practise, rehearse, anticipate actively, try out conversations;
- work in manageable achievable chunks, don't try to get everything done at once;
- undertake some early experiments which generate success and positive feedback.

---

Consideration also needs to be given to the communication of feedback, and how best to make this constructive. This raised certain principles (see Figure 7.8).

**Figure 7.8** *Principles of constructive feedback*

---

- be descriptive rather than evaluative;
- be specific;
- refer to behaviour which can be changed;
- offer alternatives, leaving the recipient with a choice;
- acknowledge with the person that the feedback you're giving is from your perspective.

---

All the materials above were at least mentioned in this important day's work, but were more properly addressed during aspects of conversations during the ensuing meetings.

## Day Four: Issues in group supervision

In this meeting we considered supervision in small groups. This theme was handled in a problem-solving style, first clarifying the issues mentors were facing in their small groups, and then sharing and developing strategies.

Asking round raised issues such as:

- three is a small group, two is even smaller!;
- these groups, like all others, are affected by their context, and social differentiators (class, race, sex, age, religion . . .);
- as in all groups an excessive focus on the leader can develop.

Group arrangements such as those shown in Figure 7.9 were identified:

**Figure 7.9** *Patterns of behaviour in small groups*

 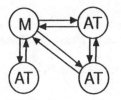 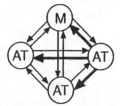

Focus on leader
little between ATs

Coalitions in a group
one member left out

Dominance
by one

In developing strategies it was fruitful to clarify how we can benefit from group rather than individual supervision (see Figure 7.10).

**Figure 7.10** *Strategies in group supervision*

- set an overall goal of learning from experience and from each other;
- give explicit attention to the contribution rates in the group;
- develop tasks for members to do together both inside the group, with or without mentor presence, and outside the group, eg exchanging experiences of the Institute, of reading they've done, investigating their views of a pupil they both teach;
- support lots of comparisons between members, such as their experiences, their evaluations;
- keep an explicit focus on both similarities and differences between group members in order to work against false consensus or easy polarisation;
- ask one group member what their perspective is on another's reported issue thus guarding against a simple 'me too' identification;
- ask one group member what they would suggest as a strategy for another;
- develop a routine for exchanging recent experiences;
- remember to rotate pairs in pairwork, and to do this even when the group is as small as four;
- in active approaches such as role-play, ensure that all take a range of roles by rotation;
- involve others such as subject mentors, or pupils, in the meetings.

By this stage in the experiment we were reaching the end of the first year of the scheme. Perhaps it was this that suggested a need for a review.

## Day Five: Reflection and review

This raised such issues as whether we were promoting the development of a reflective teacher. In the spirit of not applying to others notions we cannot apply to ourselves, we first identified when we found it possible to reflect on our work. This was extended into an analysis of features of the school, features of the teams we work in, and features of ourselves which either helped or hindered us to reflect. Figure 7.11 shows some of the matters raised.

This led us to consider the features of school which provide a productive context for school-based training. Some of the comments made are combined into the final reflections of this chapter.

**Figure 7.11** *Helping and hindering reflection*

| | Helps me reflect | Hinders my reflection |
|---|---|---|
| Aspects of my school as an organisation | culture of debate and consultation<br><br>the nature of our clientele, especially the diversity<br><br>problems and issues thrown up<br><br>processes of development planning<br><br>some Professional Development days<br><br>accepting change (again!) | overload<br><br>no resources for supporting reflection<br><br>management by senior workaholics |
| Aspects of the teams/ groups I work in | group climate, non-hierarchical<br><br>being given and asked for feedback<br><br>respect for other views<br><br>meeting in teams, with an effective meeting structure<br><br>using evidence | group concentration on petty issues<br><br>static membership to a group<br><br>differences in personal style |
| Aspects of me as a person | wanting to improve<br><br>enjoying ideas<br><br>satisfaction from problem-solving | reluctance in the face of overload<br><br>wanting an easy life<br><br>avoiding extras |

## Day Six: Focusing on difficult issues in supervision

At the time of writing, the most recent exploration has addressed the raising of 'difficult issues'. This mainly referred to occasions when a teacher in training seems not to be learning, has become 'stuck' and needs to be enabled to move on. Difficult relations which might arise in the school were also considered.

What makes one issue difficult to raise and another one not? Examples demonstrated that the raising of matters of concern becomes a problem when:

- we predict an accusation in reply;
- we view the situation as one of blame;
- we take refuge in rules;
- we feel we're 'taking sides' or are being invited to do so, especially where another colleague on the school staff is concerned;
- we forget to talk about the detail of the things that are happening here and now, and get entangled in speculation about the future;
- we feel we're going to be accused of hardheartedness, of ignoring others' problems and so on;
- we believe it won't achieve anything, such as changes to behaviour;
- we feel that people will respond with a revenge reaction;
- we overstate the extent to which our role includes protecting someone.

A key question for clarifying the important content of what we felt was a difficult issue is: Is the person learning or not? This often brings us back to the appropriate focus and legitimates a detailed examination of the issue. Guidelines which help us move forward on such occasions include:

- if we trust our judgement, make it explicit, convey it in detail, we might move on;
- we might be able to communicate our perspective without taking sides;
- we have a valuable picture which is based on various forms of data and characterised by distance, although it is incomplete;
- we can take care not to become entangled;
- we need to remember to be specific and clear;
- where conflict seems to be arising, conflict resolution consists of people communicating their various perspectives in depth;
- there are limits to the effects our interventions have on others, and we may find that we have reached the limit of our role.

## Other aspects

This account has mainly focused on the skills area of the experiment. This has been deliberate in order to make a contribution to this particular aspect of mentoring and mentor training. Some issues which have been neglected so far need to be mentioned.

The scheme of assessment in any partnership between schools and training institutions can provide an arena for tension and conflict. In the case of our ATS, the regulations had not been developed to include assessment, although the practice of assessment was developed. The recording and reporting scheme was largely devised by the school mentors. It included target setting and self-evaluation by the articled teachers, and headings under which this could be discussed with supervision. An agreed statement was then sent on to the school mentor (ie professional tutor) which included some guidelines for the future. The school mentor then forwarded an agreed statement to the Institute. It was agreed that this should operate at key points in the two-year programme, and it seems to have been effective, a fact which may reflect the level of expertise that school teachers have in formative assessment through records of achievement. Mentors have also clarified their role with respect to articled teachers assignments. These are often substantial pieces of school-based enquiry, the criteria for the assessment of which were published at the start of the course. Recalling this enabled the mentors to distinguish between their support of the teacher in this situation and their more formal role as assessor. Thus a healthy triangle was retained.

The mentors have also developed a network between themselves. This has enabled them to offer to the articled teachers a series of exchange visits to schools. These extra opportunities for observation and discussion each focus on a particular theme which is a strength of the school and an interest of the mentor. These are whole day visits which continue throughout the second year, and are linked to mentor training sessions already taking place in those schools. This arrangement seems to be an important sign of the openness of schools as sites of learning, and is a good example of the way in which schools can supplement what tutors in training institutions arrange for them.

We have not yet directly addressed the question 'Is the learning transferring?' We have occasionally addressed it through the reviews of what is happening to us, and found that we are having some success. Recollections such as *I was able to give some really difficult feedback to an articled teacher* suggest this.

## REFLECTIONS

I sometimes think that there could not have been a worse point in the history of our schools at which to try this experiment. Nevertheless we could not allow the opportunity to go by, and it has been a demanding, challenging and rewarding initiative. The task of writing this account has encouraged reflection and the identification of all the holes in the scheme.

From the start of this experiment I have been struck by the lack of time for mentors, or anyone else to reflect. This is over and above the recognition that teaching is one of the most pressurised jobs there is. Perhaps the choice of senior colleagues to fill these roles accentuates the issue, perhaps it's an additional feature of city schools – certainly I find a similar phenomenon in my work with senior colleagues on other themes. But I also believe that this situation will not improve as the reduction of resources for education continues. The overall state of our schools is one in which the occasions for structured reflection and learning are being reduced by demands to do more. I offer two implications. First there is a need to fight for 'quality time' for meeting, for reflecting upon development. This often takes place off the school site. Second, schools differ to some degree in their effectiveness at promoting reflection, and this should be a key consideration in the further development of school-based ITT. If predictions that future ITT will be funded via schools become the case, it will be necessary to develop criteria for selecting appropriate sites. Considerations should include:

- the quality of practice within schools, since this is the principal focus of professional experience and source of models
- effective support of the processes of reflection and review
- a whole-school approach to staff development at all levels – initial and in-service
- an atmosphere in the school which is conducive to school-based training in terms of receptive attitudes and a willingness to support trainees
- the presence of a suitable experienced teacher as a potential mentor
- the presence of suitable mentor support and training.

Running INSET with experienced teachers on themes with a high component of interpersonal skills is something which always concerns me. At times this experiment embodied a problem-solving style of working, not in any narrow or reactive sense of the term 'problem', but in a way which involves developing the appropriate agenda each time, structuring an exploration and exchange, and clarifying strategies which could be adapted to colleagues' circumstances. As tutor, I have experienced the continuing tension of deciding what sort of structure was appropriate. As with all work of this nature there are times when there is pressure for some bland and uncontroversial content. In the face of none of us being able to say what that content is, it has to be recognised as an anxiety which is unanswerable, and which will probably recur at key moments. As with all consultation groups, I have had my private theories. One is that when things are not going so well for the mentors, the same processes are mirrored in the group sessions.

If mentors are feeling stuck or in conflict then this can easily become injected into the quality of our meetings. Happily the opposite is also the case.

## NEXT STAGE OF THE EXPERIMENT

With the demise of the ATS, we move on to examine how much of what has been learned can be applied to the latest developments in our scheme of initial training. The whole of our very large PGCE course is moving over to an 'area-based' model in which much more extended relationships with schools in geographical groups are to be developed. The key role of link teacher may bear some similarity to that of mentor, and a support programme is being devised for them. This will no doubt turn out to be a case of working out how to do more on less. The number of students is higher; the time available is not resourced. In the face of there being no immediate funding such as that available for the ATS, the development is being supported by charity, the Paul Hamlyn Foundation.

In this training experiment the roles and processes have reflected the relatively small numbers of articled teachers per school. The role focus has been more on their school mentors (professional tutors) than on the subject mentor and the process focus has been more on the individual development of articled teachers than on the group introduction to professional issues. The balance of focus in the training does not of course necessarily reflect the balance of focus in the work itself. But it is likely that a scheme with different numbers of trainees per school (and one year rather than two) would create a different balance of focus. Perhaps we'll be developing a city version of the Oxford scheme.

A further element in the next stage is to develop distance materials for supporting the processes outlined in this chapter, and to develop a video for communicating and examining some of the skills. This is but one part of the long-term project, namely to clarify further the knowledge which is required in order to facilitate the training of a teacher. In general terms, the school-based initial training of teachers may call on the following overlapping areas of knowledge and skills:

- understanding classrooms, learning and the role of the teachers;
- understanding how practising teachers learn about classrooms;
- understanding the concerns of beginner teachers;
- understanding how adults learn;
- understanding how one adult may help another learn.

The experiment outlined in this chapter has touched upon a small number of these items.

## NOTE

1. This chapter is concerned with the training of 'school mentors' (professional tutors) from schools taking articled teachers. Since schools may have more than one articled teacher, training the school mentor rather than the usual subject mentor (supervising teacher) is in part an economy measure. The course is devised on the cascade principle. Once trained in interpersonal skills, the school mentor can both use these with the supervising teachers and encourage them to use with their trainees. This explains why there is no component on the supervision of subject methods work in this course. This is not usually the task of the professional tutor.

## BIBLIOGRAPHY

Ashton, P.M.E., Henderson, E.S., Merritt, J.E. and Mortimer, D.J. (1983). *Teacher Education in the Classroom: Initial and In-Service*. Croom Helm.

Boydell, D. (1986). Issues in Teaching Practice Supervision Research: a Review of the Literature, *Teaching & Teacher Education*, Vol. 2(2) pp. 115–25.

Calderhead, J. (ed.) (1987). *Exploring Teachers' Thinking*. Cassell.

Calderhead, J. (ed.) (1988). *Teachers' Professional Learning*. Falmer Press.

Clark, C.M. (1988). Teacher Preparation: Contributions of Research on Teacher Thinking, *Educational Researcher*, Mar, pp. 5–12.

Goldhammer, R., Anderson, R.H. and Kratjewski, R.J. (1980). *Clinical Supervision: Special Methods for the Supervision of Teachers*. Holt, Rinehart and Winston.

Hawkins, D. and Shohet, R. (1989). *Supervision in the Helping Professions*. Open University Press.

Lacey, C. (1977). *The Socialization of Teachers*. Methuen.

Lewis, H. (1990). Some Aspects of the Tutor's Role in Initial and In-service Education: in Aubrey, C. (ed.) *Consultancy in the United Kingdom: its Role and Contribution to Educational Change*. Falmer Press.

Nias, J. (1984). Learning and Acting the Roles: In-school Support for Primary Teachers. *Educational Review*. Vol. 36(1). pp. 3–15.

Partington, J. (1982). 'Teachers in School as Teaching Practice Supervisors', *Journal of Education for Teaching*. Vol. 8. pp. 262–74.

Schon, D. (1983). *The Reflective Practitioner: How Professionals Think in Action*. Basic Books/Temple Smith.

Stones, E. (1984). *Supervision in Teacher Education: a Counselling and Pedagogical Approach*. NFER-Nelson.

Stones, E. (1988). *Ritual and Reality and Psychology and Teacher Education*. Vernon-Wall Lecture, British Psychological Society.

Wragg, E.C. (1984). *A Review of Research in Teacher Education*. NFER-Nelson.

*Chapter 8*

# Initiating a Mentorship Training Programme

Alison Hill, Mike Jennings and Bryan Madgwick

## INTRODUCTION

The Articled Teacher Scheme (ATS) at West Sussex Institute of Higher Education was co-operatively developed by a regional consortium of the West Sussex Institute of Higher Education and King Alfred's College, Winchester, and the Hampshire, West Sussex, and Isle of Wight LEAs. It is the second largest such scheme in the country, with 45 primary students (30 infant/first and 15 junior/middle) and two secondary maths students in its first cohort. The mentorship training programme also currently in operation at the West Sussex Institute began in July 1990, just before the first cohort of PGCE articled teachers started their two-year course in the September.

The articled teachers are guided and supported both by a college-based tutor and his or her 'partner', a school-based teacher (the mentor). These collaborate in developing the complementary school-centred (3–4 days a week) and college-centred (1–2 days a week) programmes for the articled teacher(s) working in each school, but it is the mentor who has the major ongoing responsibility for the articled teacher's development.

The mentors are themselves supported by a two-year, college- and school-based INSET development programme which leads to two linked Certificates in Advanced Educational Studies (CAES), validated by the University of Southampton as part of a Regional Transfer Credit Scheme.

Subsequent sections of this article consider the developments and issues involved in the early planning and implementation of this mentorship training programme, which has just embarked on its second year.

## THE CONCEPT OF THE MENTOR IN THE WEST SUSSEX SCHEME

Various aspects of mentorship were discussed by the development team planning the mentorship training programme – the meaning of the word 'mentor', course content and phasing, the nature of the characteristics, role and effectiveness of the mentor, and the constraints that would also affect course design, for example. Early in our discussions we agreed on certain features in our approach: that the mentor's central involvement in the training programme was fundamental to the success of the articled teacher venture; that a clear understanding of the mentor's role was essential; that following what we were planning for the articled teachers, the mentorship programme too should include a developmental profile of competencies; and that it would be sensible if the two schemes – articled teacher and mentor – were planned and developed side by side as much as possible.

What was less clear was an obvious blueprint of mentor competencies (or indeed of a mentorship training programme) we could adopt from elsewhere, either in practice in another institution or described in the very limited literature that seemed to be available in July 1989 when we first began drafting the proposal.

We discovered later that mentorship is not a new concept in other areas and professions (for example social work, midwifery and various industrial and commercial contexts), and that there is some mentorship tradition in American teacher education. There seemed to be little extensive experience or tradition, however, in British teacher education. Only the slightly different approaches at Sussex University (the largely school-based teacher tutor scheme) and at Oxford University (the Internship Scheme) appeared to be of obvious relevance, but there was very little time to consult or visit these programmes before the submission of the proposal.

Accordingly, the development team met frequently as a self-help group with minimum recourse to outside reference. It brainstormed ideas, determined a writing schedule and agreed drafting and editing responsibilities.

It seemed to us important that the teachers who were to become the mentors (and the schools in which they taught) should be committed to a collaborative approach to the training of teachers; that mentors should be and feel an integral part of this training process; and that competence in mentorship, as in other aspects of teaching and learning, develops through doing, reflection, analysis and discussion with others who have had similar first-hand experience. Mentors would thus be responsible for supporting the articled teachers in the classroom, in partnership with other colleagues in school and the tutor responsible from college, assisting the articled teachers to become competent and reflective practitioners by the end of the training period.

We would certainly wish to emphasise here the point about teachers – whether beginning training or as mentors – achieving not merely a simple competence. As the Registrar of CNAA's Institutions and Programmes Group remarks (Wharfe, 1991, p. 11), the ATS:

> involves not just the acquisition of basic competences or classroom management skills, it also requires progressive thinking about the teaching and learning processes; about relationships between theory and practice; and about the need to acquire self-appraisal skills, the goal of which is contir ual professional enhancement.

## THE QUALIFICATIONS NEEDED TO BE A MENTOR

The discussions within and between the development team and the LEAs concerned indicated a number of criteria to guide mentor selection. Some of these were technical ones such as having a degree and at least three years' successful teaching experience, and some reflective attitudes, skills and qualities. It proved quite a daunting list to the first cohort of mentors when it was discussed with them on their initial residential course.

The qualifications also included having the confidence of senior management and colleagues within the school and LEA; an awareness of the importance of interpersonal skills, flexibility and sensitivity in meeting the articled teachers' needs; a commitment to action-enquiry, open reflective debate and the development initiatives they entailed; the ability to be assertive (and to encourage it in others), and to be articulate and analytical; the ability to assess the articled teacher's development against set criteria, but to interpret the criteria flexibly; proven leadership qualities (identified by the head and LEA), especially the ability to stimulate self-development in others through reflection and analysis; and, not least, optimism and a sense of humour.

Subsequently, H.M. Chief Inspector for Teacher Training reported some articled teachers' views of the appropriate characteristics of the mentor (Cambridge Conference, 1991). He indicated that early evaluation in the autumn of 1990 suggested that articled teachers wanted mentors who were: 'experienced, high quality teachers, flexible, approachable, authoritative, perceptive, available – and young . . .' These last two characteristics produced much merriment when they were outlined to our own mentors on one of their training days in the second term, but they were prepared to do their best . . .

## MENTOR COMPETENCIES

In drafting our profile of mentor competencies we saw the effectiveness of the mentor centred in the following areas. These are not in any way definitive and have been amended slightly for the second year of the operation of the two schemes, but they seemed to us to encompass the essential tasks involved in being an effective mentor.

1. Being responsible for establishing a supportive supervisory relationship with the articled teacher, demonstrating competency in:

- providing help and support to the articled teacher without encouraging dependence;
- encouraging personal reflection and self-appraisal in the articled teacher.

2. Applying the counselling skills necessary to become an effective helper, demonstrating competency in:

- establishing an open and trusting working relationship with the articled teacher;
- providing relevant feedback;
- exercising 'active listening' skills by creating a climate in which the articled teacher's needs and difficulties can be articulated and acted upon appropriately.

3. Developing the skills associated with teacher competence by supporting the development of effective classroom practice. For this, the mentor should be competent in assisting the articled teacher to:

- develop a sound knowledge and understanding of the curriculum;
- identify learning processes;
- set short- and long-term goals for learning and teaching;
- analyse and appraise her/his own performance;
- monitor and assess children's progress; and, in addition,
- negotiate appropriate teaching strategies and classroom-based action plans with the articled teacher.

4. Maintaining, with the college-based tutor, the articled teacher's profile and the monitoring and assessment of work in the classroom, demonstrating competency in:

- jointly identifying criteria with the articled teacher for recognising the components of effective classroom practice;
- the negotiation and communication skills necessary to compile a realistic profile of the articled teacher;
- interpreting and applying assessment criteria relating to the articled teacher's work in the classroom.

5. There was the need to inform, organise and support colleagues in becoming involved in the training programme in school in order to provide breadth and depth of experience for the articled teacher. In profile terms, the mentor should therefore demonstrate competency in:

- involving colleagues in the initiative;
- developing and co-ordinating their colleagues' contributions.

6. Identifying, with colleagues, curriculum specialisms within the school, other neighbouring schools and, where appropriate, schools in the LEA cluster area. For this area, evidence of competency would be sought in the mentor's ability to:

- plan and support specialist contributions to assist in the provision of a coherent and broad school experience;
- establish contacts and development programmes with other schools and providers.

## SUPPORTING AND DEVELOPING THE MENTOR

### The two-year part-time Certificate in Mentorship

When the initial proposal for an articled teacher programme was being developed, we argued that a parallel support course for the mentor was essential, for the successful development of the entire scheme. We further argued that it was sensible to design this support programme as an award-bearing, 120 hour INSET course. This would be another strand in the range of Certificates and Diplomas in Advanced Education Studies offered by the Institute and validated by the University of Southampton as part of the regional CATS programme. Teachers do an enormous amount of complex, skilled and undervalued work and its worth and importance is highlighted by validated qualifications in this way. It would not be compulsory to register for this CAES in Mentorship, but in the event 33 out of 36 mentors have taken up the option, and should gain their Certificate at the end of the two years, at the same time as the articled teachers gain their PGCE.

# THE MENTORSHIP PROGRAMME: COURSE CONTENT

## The three-day residential introductory course

The programme began with a three-day residential course at the Institute in mid-July 1990, before the articled teachers began their placement in the mentors' schools in September. The majority of our longer in-service courses in teacher education – the MA(Ed), the in-service BEd/BA(Ed)(Hons) and our Mathematics INSET courses – begin with a residential element. We feel it is a powerful way of clarifying and establishing course intentions and learning and teaching approaches, and encouraging the team building that should ensure a minimum of problems later in the course – not that some communication and misunderstanding difficulties do not occur; far from it.

The residential course was designed with an emphasis on two areas that seemed to us sensible and important at this stage of the programme. The first was an introduction to the structure and intentions of both the Articled Teacher and Mentorship programmes (and their relation to the current context of teacher education). The second area was consideration of the nature and development of a positive, supportive relationship between the mentor and the beginner teacher.

Sessions focused on introductions to each other; consideration of the qualities, characteristics and role of the mentor; interpersonal skills, including listening, counselling, and the building of personal and team relationships; the profile of competencies, both that for the articled teacher and that for the mentor; the nature of supervision; and the planning of an induction programme for the first team, and particularly the first week, of the placements.

These areas were explored through case studies, role play, small-group discussion, video analysis and input lectures. A further aspect was an encouragement to develop informal area groupings of mentors, to meet regularly in one of the mentor's schools or at a Professional Centre, and to discuss and support each other in their experience of mentorship and exploration of its nature and role.

## The Institute-based day release element

Following the residential course, the mentors attend two INSET days at the Institute each term, one at the beginning and one at the end of term. These have been a deliberate mixture of two features. One element is inputs by course tutors – on, for example, time management; the need and strategies for non-threatening assertiveness; developing adults' rather than the children's learning they are familiar with; arrangements and guidelines for the triangular end of term profile meetings of mentor, articled teacher and professional tutor; and developments in the mentorship field nationally.

The other element is the provision of sessions which are opportunities for mentors to bring problems, questions and issues to the days for discussion and resolution, and to meet with professional tutors. Each day also ends with a plenary, discussing any issues arising from the day, clarifying and sorting out administrative and other confusions, and confirming or amending the draft programme for the next INSET day. The emphasis in these days is always on meeting the mentors' needs and requests as they explore their role at different phases in the course. They are encouraged at all times to help determine the agenda, with tutors creating the opportunities and providing the inputs to facilitate their development.

## The school-based elements

As well as these nine whole INSET days in college over the two years, there is the equivalent of one day a term which is designed as a school-based opportunity for the mentor, professional tutor and articled teacher to work together. This might consist of discussions between all three, or between any two of the three, or an opportunity for the mentor and professional tutor jointly to observe and discuss the articled teacher at work in the classroom. It will also include the end of term profile meeting, when the three will come together to review the articled teacher's progress formally, and determine the action plan for the next phase or term.

The final part of this school-based component in the Mentorship Programme is two hours per term of tutorial support from the professional tutor. This centres on discussion of the mentor's own Profile of Competencies (the ongoing log of events, issues, questions and the articled teacher's development kept by the mentor), and anything else of significance that relates to the mentorship role.

One final point here is that throughout the structure and content of the training programme there has been a commitment to the notion of 'ownership' by the mentors. This seems to us important, and we have consistently sought to encourage all those participating to become fully committed and involved in the development of the programme.

## Assessing the mentor

As was mentioned earlier, the course development team felt it appropriate that there should be common elements in the programmes experienced by the articled teacher and the mentor. Thus, we have tried to ensure that some of the same tutors worked on both programmes, and that there will be opportunities for the trios of articled teachers, mentors and professional tutors to meet occasionally on college-based days. More significantly, both have the same length of course, the mix of college- and school-based sessions, certificated (if differently so) courses and a consequent assessment process.

Just as the articled teacher's development was in part assessed by a Profile of Competencies and an ongoing file, so too would the mentor's be. Thus, for all mentors registered for the CAES, formative assessment is undertaken through a Profile of Competencies, and maintenance and completion of a 10,000 word or equivalent Personal Log/Journal. Those mentors who choose not to register for the Certificate (normally because they are already engaged in another award-bearing course or have a new and major development responsibility in school) are still required to attend the full number of training days and maintain an ongoing log/journal which is reflective and analytical in nature.

## MENTORSHIP: KEY ISSUES

A fundamental concern in our early development discussions was to create a clear, detailed and principled rationale for the two complementary programmes, but one which was open-ended and flexible enough to be an enabling rather than a constraining framework. There was little previous direct experience for any of us to work from, and we were conscious of constructing a complex structure of interrelationships (schools, HE institutions and LEAs; articled teachers, mentors and other teachers, and professional tutors) that would need considerable administrative and organisational skill to realise.

There were clearly going to be problems, needs and confusions that we had not foreseen at all – such as the depth and importance of the *emotional* dimension of the relationships involved, particularly the mentor/articled teacher relationship, or the need to focus on the nature of adult/adult relationships as well as adult/children relationships. There would also be ones we could now glimpse but dimly in these early planning stages – such as what might happen when a mentor leaves during the course, or there is a breakdown in relationships. There would also be others we might foresee but could do little or nothing about at that stage – such as ensuring sufficiently generous time allowances for professional tutors to visit schools, or planning the content of college-based sessions to complement what was taking place in schools.

Reviewing our experience now, nearly two years on from our first discussions and after experiencing the first year of both the Articled Teacher and Mentorship Programmes, we want to identify a number of issues we see as significant. The mentor/articled teacher relationship relates more to the nature of mentorship itself, and this is considered at some length. Other issues highlight aspects of the introduction and operation of a mentorship training programme such as the one we and others are currently engaged in. There is, though, considerable intersection between these two main areas.

## The mentor/articled teacher relationship

Building a positive and effective relationship – one that is going to last for at least two years in our scheme, and involves assessment as well as information, guidance and counselling – is often difficult, even with goodwill and understanding on both sides.

One of the mentor's initial responsibilities is to clarify the characteristics and intentions of the roles and relationship as she or he understands them, and to discuss these with the articled teacher. Even when both sides have received induction training and supporting documentation, there is still scope for misunderstanding and uncertainty as well as misperception, especially if the role and intentions are unfamiliar territory to the mentor – and for the mentors in such a pilot scheme this year they have been.

Second, the mentor and articled teacher do not choose each other, though every effort was made by the LEA in our case to match up complementary interests and approaches. This attempt at matching was done by encouraging the articled teachers to visit a number of participating schools before final placement, and to indicate a preference (schools and mentors were also able to indicate a preference for the articled teachers they saw). Even so, there is necessarily a period of getting to know each other when the articled teacher begins the placement, and this might result in like or dislike, and consequent decisions and developments about positive working/social relations. As in a strained marriage, especially an arranged one, two years is a long time to be living/working together if – emotionally, philosophically, culturally or politically – you find yourself at odds or become estranged.

Third, there is an emotional dimension to the relationships, which can involve strong feelings and thoughts about each other, and the powerful effects this dimension has should not be underestimated. The two participants are bound together in a very intense and long-term professional relationship – very new and different for both – and teaching is a highly complex and pressurised context in which this takes place.

Various problems can arise here. For the articled teacher, the mentor is an assessor (for many articled teachers this is likely to be a negative characteristic) as well as a supporter and guide (desired and positive). When the articled teacher is clearly not showing the development or attitude expected by the programme, it is usually the mentor who has to initiate discussion about such shortcomings, and several have found it quite difficult to broach the subject. Partly this has been because the mentors do feel the major emphasis in their approach is to be positive and encouraging rather than critical. Partly, though, it has been because of a feeling that if the articled teacher is not doing well it is because the mentor herself/himself is not doing the mentoring job well enough. There have been tears shed and guilt felt by both sides in a number of relationships in our own scheme this year, relationships usually – but not always – successfully re-established after some painful negotiation.

A related and important aspect of this is the question of assertiveness, and the need for all the participants, whether mentors, articled teachers or others, to be more assertive about their feelings, reservations and wishes without being in any way negative or threatening. Some mentors have been reticent about doing this, either for the reasons outlined above or because they have been giving the articled teacher every possible opportunity to show evidence of progress and understanding not yet forthcoming.

Understandable though this is, this reticence has led to difficulties in a few cases. There have been several articled teachers who would have benefited from much more open, direct and early guidance and instruction, and others who have taken up an enormous amount of time for all concerned – the whole school staff, also the college tutor and second opinion tutors – because the mentor was less assertive than she or he should have been, even though this was a criterion involved in their selection. Admittedly, though, the balance can be a delicate one, and hindsight a great teacher. What has resulted is that the issue of assertiveness has been raised several times in the mentor training days, and pair and small-group simulations used to help mentors develop confidence and skills in the area.

A fourth issue here is that the relationship is also a changing one. The growth in feeling at ease with each other, in developing mutual regard, is one aspect that should be developing – being able to joke with each other, recognising and accepting each other's strengths and weaknesses, enjoyment in collaborating on different tasks.

What is also changing, however, is the articled teacher's professional competence and insight, and the reduction in need for direction from the mentor. Parelleling what should be taking place between teacher and children over their year in the classroom together, the articled teacher becomes more an independent learner, taking her or his place alongside the mentor and other staff as a colleague rather than as an 'apprentice'. It will be a reflection of the personal and professional strength, sensitivity and insight that has developed in the partnership that it can recognise and promote such development.

The fifth issue is the question of the school's and mentor's expectations of what the articled teacher ought to be doing and demonstrating. Several articled teachers have remarked that their schools seem to see them as qualified staff already, and expect them to take on full class and team responsibilities, especially in the second and third terms of the final year. There is evidence from some mentor and headteacher comments halfway through Term 4 that this does seem to be the case; the clear distinction between students in training and graduates with QTS appears to be blurred in some schools. Articled teachers' needs for study, planning, preparation, evaluation, marking and display time – crucial for *all* students in training – are seen as a luxury by some, especially when many schools are feeling overwhelmed by the pressures of trying to implement so many new initiatives, and seek all hands to the plough.

The other aspect of this is the perception by schools, LEAs and institutions that this first cohort of articled teachers is of a high quality – because of such factors as the lengthy selection, interviewing and matching process, the commitment of the applicants themselves, and the positive attitude engendered in all those taking part in a pilot scheme. Expectations in turn are therefore also high; articled teachers *should* be able to take full class and team responsibilities from an early stage some feel.

Last, there is the question of the number of articled teachers a mentor can effectively supervise while still successfully maintaining a high-quality approach. In our scheme it was agreed that the LEAs would decide the details of the placements of articled teachers and the selection of mentors. In the majority of schools in the first year a mentor was responsible for two articled teachers, but in a large number of cases it was only one, and in only two cases was the mentor responsible for three articled teachers.

There are a number of drawbacks to having other than a 1:1 ratio, and most of the participants in the scheme felt that these outweighed any advantages. The intensity of the relationship, the unfamiliarity of the role, the need to organise time in other classrooms, the demands on the mentor's time and the considerable all-round pressures being faced by schools were all issues emphasised in formative and end-of-year evaluation that indicated that a 1:1 ratio should be the norm for the new cohort starting in September 1991; and that has duly been implemented.

This is obviously, though, a very costly approach, and one not likely to survive the pilot period. The national survey of the ATS undertaken by NFER (1991), and the 'thinking aloud' currently being done at various levels of the government and DES confirm this. One suggestion from H.M. Inspectorate, for example, has been that mentors might supervise up to six or seven students at any one time. Certainly, this cost versus effectiveness issue is one likely to be at the centre of the debate for the foreseeable future – as it is in the education debate in general.

## Issues arising from implementing a mentor training programme

*Adults working with other adults*

The importance of the fact that mentors were working intensively in a different way with other adults – as opposed to children – did not really dawn on us, as mentors or college tutors, until we were discussing issues and experiences with others at the Cambridge Conference on Mentor Training in January 1991. Mentors had been selected (by the LEA) because they appeared to have all sorts of appropriate interpersonal skills, leadership qualities and positive attitudes. These, however, were with colleagues, and on a 'co-equals' basis which did not involve assessment. The great bulk of their experience in counselling, assessment and 'supervision' was with children. It seemed that this might relate at least in part to the question of assertiveness discussed earlier, and the topic was raised and considered in training day sessions in the second term. It has now been built in to the residential element at the very start of the programme for Cohort 2.

*Payment for mentors*

There has been some debate nationally about the question of payment for mentors, and the issue of payment for this potentially very influential role was discussed with the LEAs involved in our scheme at the beginning of the planning process. There are several aspects to the debate. For example, should mentors be paid at all and if so, how much should they receive? Should other colleagues involved in the training programme receive payment, and on what basis should this be worked out? And, if a whole school approach is being urged, should not any payment go to the school rather than to an individual?

In the end it was agreed that payment would go to the mentor alone (each would be paid around £550 for an articled teacher, with around another £125 for any additional one) because it would involve them more than anyone else in extra hours and responsibilities, and should be recognised as a new and important post within a school. It could become part of teachers' career development structure in a similar way to other allowances. Although we have reservations about certain of Mary Warnock's suggestions for a wholesale move to school-based education, with training establishments concentrating only on research, administration and validation (Warnock, 1990, p. 18), we agree with much of her view that:

> one of the great advantages of the mentor system would be its effect on the professionalism of teachers in school. Becoming a mentor would be one possible way forward for successful and ambitious teachers who at present can aim only at headships. To become a mentor in a teaching school would be to achieve a different kind of eminence. Mentors would exert influence over a wide field, affecting not only individual students, but also teaching methods and content. They would, in fact become the most directly influential figures in school education . . . and [it] would keep many excellent teachers in the classroom.

*The need for a whole-school approach*
The need for a whole-school approach to this initiative – as with other current initiatives such as curriculum planning, assessment and community involvement – was recognised by most of the participating schools from the outset. The whole staff discussed it and agreed an outline programme in which the mentor took the co-ordinating role, keeping the staff informed about developments and ensuring that they had the opportunity to participate in planning and evaluating the work. They recognised, as Wharfe comments, (op. cit., p. 11) that, 'The presence of a . . . mentor can itself . . . help promote the school's own educational thinking and dynamic, and so enhance the learning of the whole institution.' This whole-school involvement helped to offset the anxieties and teething troubles experienced more keenly by those schools that did not adopt a whole-school approach, and schools participating this time round were much encouraged to do so.

There are two other related issues here. One is the movement of mentors to other schools because of promotion or other reasons during the course, and this happened in several cases during the first year. It is unfortunate if this happens, but unavoidable, and there did seem to be evidence that the promotions had partly been a consequence of the mentoring experience. The possibility of this kind of situation had been discussed at the planning stage, and schools had already identified another member of staff who would take over the mentor role if this should occur, illustrating the importance of the whole-school approach again.

The other reason for having all staff in the school involved from the earliest point is that most, if not all, will be involved in the articled teacher's development programme at some point in the two years, and need to be aware of the intentions, schedule, responsibilities and best approaches involved in having one in their classroom. In one case where there were two articled teachers in the school, one was attached to the mentor's class and one to another teacher. Unfortunately, the head, who was retiring, had not consulted or kept all the staff informed about plans for the start of term in the autumn and the teacher concerned felt both confused and annoyed at her sudden and unexpected involvement in the scheme.

## Time

Time is an eternal problem for us all. There is never enough of it, and it is difficult to manage it efficiently when you are subject to a host of competing demands. Time was needed for meetings between the mentor and the articled teacher, on a weekly, and initially a daily, basis; for the mentor to discuss and plan placements with other colleagues; for the mentor to maintain her or his ongoing log; for the tutor from college to visit the school for meetings with the articled teacher and the mentor both separately and together; for the end of term Profile Meeting; and for everyone to plan activities and sessions in classroom and college.

And all this was happening in a context of SATS being undertaken for the first time, SIMS training, revised National Curriculum documents, school development plans, INSET days, parents' evenings and carol concerts, with staff appraisal to come . . .

We are sure there has been no more satisfactory resolution of the time issue in our scheme than anywhere else. Sessions on the mentor training days addressed the topic of work pressures, stress and time management, and offered strategies to help alleviate such problems in school – but the time management session itself usually ran over time into the next session.

## Logistics, communication and timetabling

This has proved to be a major area of difficulty for the college end of the scheme, particularly as it has been the HE Institute in our scheme that has taken the lead in drafting the original proposal and designing and co-ordinating most of the two courses. The problems of staffing and timetabling the college-based sessions, clarifying intentions and guide-lines and communicating such information to all participants have been complex. The attempt has taken place at a time of increased student numbers in the Institute's BEd programme, and simultaneous imple-mentation of a number of new initiatives on campus, such as the development of a Primary Education Centre.

The information concerned must also go to two institutions and their tutors (King Alfred's College, Winchester, as well as the Institute), three LEAs, about 25 schools, 35 mentors and 45 articled teachers, and reach them all at the same time and be interpreted in the same way; and now there is a second cohort of both articled teachers and mentors . . .

*Are these initiatives more successful than traditional ways of training?*
This brings us to the final issue we have identified. It raises questions about the worth of the ATS and the supporting Mentor Training Programme. There is as yet no clearly discernible agreement or definition about what constitutes 'quality' or the best means of achieving it, in classrooms either in schools or colleges. There is a passionate debate going on about initial teacher education and extensive media coverage of the rumours, possibilities, claims and occasional proposals that together cloud its future picture.

Early signals from both the participants and external evaluators such as NFER (1991, op.cit.) suggest a successful beginning to these two initiatives, albeit with certain qualifications. Not least as positive evidence is the ability of the central participants – articled teachers, mentors and college-based tutors – and the central partners – schools, LEAs and HE institutions – to articulate their enthusiasm and commitment for both ventures. There do seem grounds for cautious optimism about the quality of insight, performance, commitment and understanding in both the beginner teachers and those involved in their mentorship in such school-based work.

Difficult though it is to predict them with any certainty, however, new government policies may attempt to do two things. First, they may try to increase dramatically the proportion of school-based work for all BEd and PGCE students without noting the likely effects of such overload on schools – and the question of whether there are enough 'good practice' schools and teachers to support this massive influx is a question that has not yet had proper consideration, let alone an answer.

Second, and simultaneously, any policy change will certainly seek to reduce the comparatively generous resources and financial support initiatives such as the ATS has enjoyed. They are too expensive. And disturbingly, these moves are likely to take place in a climate that will continue to underestimate the importance of reflection, analysis and theoretical understanding of teaching and learning in improving the quality of education. And yet it is these aspects of training that are asked for more of rather than less of by the articled teachers and mentors we have worked with.

Whether the undoubted current enthusiasm for school/college partnerships and school-based initiatives will be sustained if such developments take place remains an open question. As David Blake has pointed out (1990, pp. 370-1):

The location of teacher training in schools is unlikely to be a panacea. There are good grounds for believing that the location of training is less significant than the process which results from the interrelationship of its parts. What is needed is clarity about the functions of the different aspects of training and their identification within a hierarchy of professional learning ... All participants in training need their own staff development, time off from their own practice so that they can engage in training and clarity about respective functions. A move to more school-based forms of training is unlikely to be cheap.

## CONCLUSIONS

Overall then, our own and national evaluation by both participants and observers suggests that the Articled Teacher Schemes and the associated Mentorship Training Programmes, like those at West Sussex Institute, are functioning successfully. There have been (and will continue to be) some limitations, weaknesses and surprises in such a pilot scheme, as well as strengths, and we have tried to identify the key issues that are engaging us as we work through our own scheme. The insights that have been gained over the first year have led to some re-emphasis and minor amendment to the programmes designed for the second cohorts of both groups that started in September 1991, and doubtless there will be further such changes for Cohort 3 in September 1992.

We are, though, convinced that for all the qualifications that might be made about them, these partnership initiatives that unite both initial and in-service teacher education are essential and appropriate for the professional development of all teachers. Whatever further transformations happen in the teacher education field here over the next ten years – and we certainly see a significant growth in mentorship and supporting training programmes for the next three years at least – our experience in the West Sussex schemes leaves us very positively committed to the concept of mentorship in a school/higher education/LEA partnership.

## REFERENCES

Blake, D. (1990). 'The teacher training debate: some parallels from health and social work', *Journal of Education Policy*. Vol. 5(4).
NFER. (1991). 'Evaluation of the Articled Teachers Scheme: Executive Summary'. Windsor. National Foundation for Education Research.
Warnock, M. (1990). 'Trained Relations', *Times Educational Supplement*. 21.9.1990.

West Sussex Institute of Higher Education. (1990–1). *Articled Teacher Scheme: The CNAA Validated Document; Student Handbook; Mentor Handbook (1991); First Conference of Headteachers and Mentors (Conference Report).*

Wharfe, L. (1991). 'A new approach to teacher training', *Higher Education News.* No. 13 Spring 1991.

# PART III  Three Examples of Mentoring in Practice

## Chapter 9

# Collaborative Teaching

Katharine Burn

## INTRODUCTION

This chapter focuses on a very specific aspect of the mentoring role, exploring one particular technique that mentors can use in helping beginning teachers learn to teach. This technique may be defined as 'collaborative teaching', but since this term is capable of a wide variety of interpretations further clarification is needed. Collaborative teaching here means any lesson that is jointly planned and jointly taught by a mentor (or experienced teacher) and a beginning teacher, hereafter referred to as 'intern'. (This term is used within Oxford University's PGCE course – the Internship Scheme. It is borrowed from the training of medical students in teaching hospitals and is intended to highlight the status of trainee teachers within the school community, and to indicate the extent of the partnership between school and university in their training.)

The degree of collaboration involved in the process may vary considerably. The mentor may plan the lesson outline and then suggest a specific slot within it for which he or she would like the intern to take responsibility; or, at the other end of the spectrum, both mentor and intern may plan the whole lesson 'from scratch' together. However, a collaborative lesson is one that has been planned to ensure that the intern has a clearly defined responsibility within it, which is deliberately targeted to help his or her learning.

The chapter is based partly on my own experience as a mentor within the Internship Scheme run by Oxford University Department of Educational Studies (OUDES), and partly on research data collected by OUDES as a prelude to the preparation of mentor training materials.[1] Interns on the scheme divide their time between school and university for the first part of the year, spending two days a week in school from October to January, and then a block of time in school from January to May. I have acted as a mentor to three pairs of history interns over the last three years, and have found collaborative teaching a very valuable way of helping interns to learn various kinds of skills, especially in the early stages of learning to teach. During last year I tried to monitor my own use of collaborative teaching, noting the reasons why I have used this technique at any particular point, and recording both the planning and evaluation of lessons that I taught jointly with an intern. I asked two other history mentors to collect similiar data from their collaborative teaching with interns, and a science and an English mentor were also tape-recorded planning and evaluating collaborative teaching, and interviewed about their use of this approach.[2] This chapter, therefore, while reflecting largely my own practice, also draws on the experiences of four other mentors, and on advice received from a variety of mentors within the Internship Scheme who commented on a draft specification of the skill of collaborative teaching that was to form the basis of mentor training materials.

## WHY DO IT?

Our experience suggests that collaborative teaching can prove a highly effective means of helping interns to develop a variety of new skills or understanding. Three important kinds of learning which are possible through collaborative teaching are:

1. learning to plan lessons carefully through being involved in joint planning with an experienced teacher, finding out what the teacher takes account of, and identifying with the planning and its consequences;
2. learning certain skills of classroom teaching through having responsibility for a specified component of the lesson, while identifying with the whole lesson and recognising the relationship of the part to the whole;
3. gaining access to the teacher's craft knowledge[3] through observation of the teacher's actions, informed by a thorough knowledge of the planning, and probably through discussion of the lesson afterwards, with a heightened awareness because of having joint responsibility for the lesson.

## Planning

Because experienced teachers do not always produce explicit plans for their lessons, interns may mistakenly assume that they too 'do not need to plan'. Collaborative teaching may be a way of making the mentor's plan more explicit, and therefore accessible to the intern. It may also demonstrate the necessity of careful planning. In planning with the intern, the mentor can also share his or her knowledge of the particular class and context; for example, the mentor's estimate of how long a suggested task might take different individuals, so reminding the intern of the need to plan extension activities for some. Even where departments have clearly defined schemes of work and sets of prepared resources to accompany these, collaborative teaching with a mentor can usefully show an intern how an experienced teacher fleshes out an outline plan, and adapts resources to the particular context in which a topic is to be taught.

## Learning skills of classroom teaching

In the early stages of training, collaborative teaching can offer the intern a protected environment in which to begin developing the skills of classroom teaching. First, by teaching alongside the intern, the mentor can remove some of the fear about maintaining discipline. Second, by taking responsibility for certain parts of the lesson, the mentor can allow the intern to concentrate on and practise specific aspects of teaching and so build up his or her confidence. The opportunity this provides for interns to focus on particular aspects is very valuable in a course built on the principles of progression and partnership.[4] One of the aims of the Internship Scheme was to avoid the experience of beginning teachers being 'flung into the deep end'. Teaching is an extremely complex skill, but it can be learned more easily if beginning teachers are introduced gradually to some of the separate components of which it is composed. Collaborative teaching allows interns to take on some aspects of the teaching task, without being obliged to tackle them all at once. They can then build on their positive achievements in one area to master more complicated techniques. It also allows for co-ordination between the partners involved in the training process. If interns are learning about certain aspects of teaching within their curriculum programme, then carefully planned joint lessons can allow them to explore those specific aspects in their own teaching. Because they do not have to take responsibility for the whole lesson they can look much more critically and thoughtfully at the same ideas in practice that they have been exploring from a more theoretical perspective.

## Gaining access to teachers' craft knowledge

Having planned the lesson with the mentor, the intern should be acutely aware of the objectives of those parts of the lesson taught by the mentor, and should therefore be more able to understand and appreciate the means that the mentor is using to achieve them. This can help to focus their observation, and alert them to particular techniques used by the mentor. They will also obviously be aware of any adaptations that the mentor may make to the agreed plan. For example, if the early parts of a lesson run on longer than anticipated, the mentor may have to replan the ending or condense the remaining material. The intern will only be aware of such changes because of his or her involvement in the planning, and this awareness can lead to fruitful discussions about how the mentor identifies priorities, or achieves objectives in a shorter time. Obviously changes can only be made if they are not going to disrupt parts of the lesson for which an intern is responsible, but surprisingly, a number of mentors have suggested that collaborative teaching is a very effective way of helping interns both to appreciate the need for flexibility, and to understand how such replanning can be done.

## THE BENEFITS FOR THE PUPILS

Part of the reason why I so enjoy working with interns, and one of the indirect benefits of collaborative teaching, are the opportunities presented by having two teachers in a classroom. It can allow for a much more lively or challenging presentation of information or ideas, using role-play or debate, for example. It can make the management of learning activities much smoother; one teacher can take on responsibility for distributing resources while the other explains the task. It can increase the amount of individual attention and support that pupils receive, and can facilitate assessment or the setting of differentiated tasks.

### An example: the sinking of the *Lusitania*

A specific example may serve to illustrate some of the benefits that can be derived from collaborative teaching. I taught the following lesson with an intern during November 1990. After an initial period of observation (three weeks in schools near their homes) and a two-week induction, the interns begin the series of 'joint' weeks, spending two days a week in school and the rest of their time at OUDES. This lesson therefore took place at a very early stage of the intern's training, during the fourth of the 'joint' weeks. It was the second time that the intern had taken any responsibility for classroom teaching.

The class we were training was a mixed ability group of 30 Year 9 pupils who were studying the First World War. The specific focus of this lesson was the German sinking of the *Lusitania*, and pupils were being asked to evaluate conflicting evidence to work out whether the ship was a 'legitimate' target. We planned the lesson a week in advance, after the intern had been able to observe me teaching the same group, and the eventual plan that we produced as as follows:

1. INTERN    Settle the class and call register. Question-and-answer to provide a recap on the previous lesson's work – the factual details of how and when the ship was sunk, and the British press reports of the sinking as 'the foulest act of murder'.

2. MENTOR    Interruption to challenge this interpretation.

3. INTERN AND MENTOR    Structured argument, with intern and mentor alternating to present different claims, each based on a specific piece of primary evidence.
*Intern* – representing the British viewpoint that the *Lusitania* was an innocent passenger ship unjustly attacked.
*Mentor* – representing the German viewpoint that the *Lusitania* was carrying arms and thus a legitimate target.

4. MENTOR    Explain the pupils' task is to analyse each piece of evidence, completing a chart to indicate exactly what each piece of evidence was, what it claimed, and whether or not it was reliable.

5. INTERN AND MENTOR    Distribute sheets of evidence and outline charts to pupils. Circulate to help or advise individual pupils as necessary.

6. MENTOR    Sum up: both sides had very different perceptions of the same event; both sought to exploit it for their own advantage.

7. INTERN    Set homework – to design a propaganda poster from either the British or the German perspective, using the sinking to justify their own position, and to recruit support.

As this lesson came so near the beginning of the intern's training, I exercised quite tight control over the planning to try to ensure that the eventual form of the lesson would provide certain specific opportunities. The focus of the OUDES curriculum programme during that particular week was on language (pupil *and* teacher talk). I was therefore determined that the intern's role in the lesson should involve her in some question-and-answer and should include a short section of exposition. I was also concerned, as was she, that during the previous week she had had a very discouraging experience with a class; in trying to conduct a session of question-and-answer she had encountered a sea of blank faces, and had felt obliged to provide the answers to her own questions. We were both anxious, therefore, to ensure that she had a positive experience of questioning, and felt able to establish some kind of rapport with the class.

To achieve these aims I steered the planning very deliberately, so that the lesson would begin with a recap based on question-and-answer (1). Because it was only a short section of the lesson we were able to concentrate on it. We could discuss in detail exactly what information the pupils would need to remember in order to tackle the next exercise, and could then work out very specifically what questions she would have to ask in order to elicit that information. We could also discuss the various ways in which these questions could be phrased to help ensure that their meaning was clear, and that the pupils understood exactly what was being asked of them. Because the planning was so detailed, it gave the intern the opportunity to learn from my experience of different types of question. It also encouraged her to plan very precisely (in the early stages of learning to teach) to ensure that she did not dry up, or encounter a discouraging silence in the face of inappropriately phrased questions. The fact that the question-and-answer was serving as a recap also gave the intern confidence that the pupils would be able and willing to respond.

The intern's surprise and obvious pleasure at the clear and accurate responses she received made the investment of time in the planning very worthwhile. The value of our discussion about specific questions was also made clear by the next lesson that the intern taught, when she specifically asked for feedback on her use of language, as to whether her questions and explanations were appropriately pitched for the age and ability of the group.

The structured debate (3) was intended to help the intern develop the skill of exposition. She was aware of a tendency in herself to 'ramble', and I hoped that the idea of an argument based on specific pieces of evidence would serve to focus her explanations. In arguing against someone else, she would have to speak clearly, and emphasise the key points. The debate was also intended to provide a more stimulating lesson for the pupils. We hoped that we could exploit the fact that there were two of us in the classroom to clarify for the pupils the nature of propaganda and to highlight the problems that historians have in reconciling contradictory accounts. I also hoped that it might encourage the intern, still at this early stage, to appreciate some of the more dynamic possibilities available for presenting material, and to have some fun with the pupils by taking on their teacher in an 'argument'.

Because the intern was not presenting the different interpretations on her own, she did not have to carry the burden of maintaining discipline and keeping the pupils' attention. I could intervene if necessary (which it was not) to reprimand pupils without undermining the intern, and yet she was able to relax from worry about discipline and concentrate on the specific task of exposition.

As well as enjoying the debate, the intern also found that assuming a role, and being able to feed off the mentor's arguments gave her more confidence in front of the class, and helped her in assuming the 'role' of a teacher (ie recognising the element of performance in teaching).

The task that we were intending to set the pupils (4) was quite a complex one, and we therefore decided that I should take this part of the lesson to allow the intern an opportunity to observe explanation and task-setting.

Having two of us available to distribute worksheets (5) and give individual help obviously benefited the pupils. It also allowed the intern an opportunity to work with individuals, to gain an understanding of their views of historical evidence, and to appreciate the nature of their thinking in working out whether sources were reliable.

The intern's observation of the 'summing up' (6), a very short section of teaching, enabled her to focus on my own use of question-and-answer. It led to a thoughtful discussion about how an experienced teacher plans questions, and how much room they leave to respond to the particular interests or ability of individuals in the class. Through the planning and teaching of the early part of the lesson she had been made aware of her own current need to clarify her teaching objectives, and to plan specifically to meet these. Her observation and the subsequent discussion allowed her to recognise some of the techniques a teacher can use in questioning to probe pupils' understanding, and how sometimes the pupils' own interests or enthusiasm can move the discussion beyond the teacher's initial objectives.

Setting the homework (7) was again a clearly defined task for the intern to take on, but one which could also allow some freedom for her to develop her own ideas. The particular homework was chosen in response to her own suggestions, as she had mentioned several examples of propaganda that she knew of relating to this event. She collected these herself and independently planned how to use them to introduce the homework to the pupils. She thus brought into the lesson valuable resources unknown to me.

## PROBLEMS AND PRACTICAL CONSTRAINTS

The above example while indicating some of the benefits of collaborative teaching also highlights many of the practical difficulties involved. Interviews with mentors practising collaborative teaching revealed further problems. First, one or two suggested that working with interns in this way can prove very threatening to both parties. Many experienced teachers have become used to working on their own without other adults around and it can be very unsettling for them to try to share 'their' class with another teacher. Interns, not surprisingly, can feel threatened by an experienced teacher in the classroom with them, feeling that the teacher's presence and contribution to the lesson are undermining their own role.

Having two 'teachers' sharing responsibility for a lesson may also cause considerable confusion. Pupils may be uncertain about who is 'in charge', and this may serve to undermine an intern's confidence if the pupils consistently look to the 'proper' teacher for help. Having the mentor there may even encourage the intern to relax and leave things to the mentor, at times when they should really be taking responsibility for the lesson.

Another difficulty can be ensuring that there is adequate liaison between the mentor and intern during a lesson. Even the best laid plans may need adaptation, and it can be difficult and potentially unsettling to have to change course part way through a lesson. It is not always easy to ensure that there are reasonable opportunities for liaison without these appearing to the pupils as mere occasions for 'teacher chat'!

The aspect of collaborative teaching that mentors have found most problematic, however, is that of time. Joint planning is extremely time-consuming; any lesson would probably require at least an hour's planning (the above example took an hour to plan), and, if the intern is to derive the maximum benefit from it, time will also be needed afterwards to discuss the lesson together. Few mentors could find this sort of time to devote to a single lesson on a regular basis.

## OVERCOMING THE PROBLEMS

Collaborative teaching, as the term implies requires a high degree of co-operation between the mentor and intern. Obviously it will not work if the mentor is unhappy with the idea of working in this way. However the OUDES Internship model and other partnership and mentoring schemes have shown that a great many teachers are very keen to work alongside beginning teachers and to share their expertise with them. (Mentors who were interviewed about their use of collaborative teaching suggested that experienced teachers *might* find this kind of approach threatening, but it was clear that they personally did not.)

Where mentors are willing to expose their own practice in this way, the interns can be encouraged to find collaboration less threatening by working in this way from the very beginning of their training. Planning and teaching together with their mentor even on an occasional basis can also help them to regard their mentor as a colleague and not merely as someone there to assess their performance.

The problem of confusion over roles within the lesson can only be overcome by very thorough planning. It is essential that both mentor and intern understand their respective roles, and in particular are clear about how any transitions are to be made. Uncertainty about who is doing what, and when, will inevitably lead to confusion, especially for the pupils. Ultimately it is the mentor's responsibility to ensure that the plan and timing of the lesson are clear, and that both know who is responsible for class discipline at any particular time. This must be agreed to ensure that the intern does not abdicate certain responsibilities to the mentor, or end up feeling undermined. Despite the time involved in such detailed planning, it generally proves to be a more positive experience for the intern to plan jointly with the mentor in the early stages of the year, than to begin by drafting their own plans which have to be modified when shown to the mentor.

It is helpful if the lesson plan can include opportunities during the lesson for the mentor and intern to discuss aspects of the teaching. The intern may want to ask about something he or she has just seen the mentor do; the mentor may want to offer brief feedback on the intern's teaching, or offer guidance on the next stage of the lesson, given the way in which the class has responded so far. This kind of discussion can be a very valuable part of the process; it is one of the strengths of collaborative teaching that it can allow this kind of immediate feedback, while the events are still fresh in the mind. However, it is important to keep such discussions brief, and, if possible, to plan for them at moments when pupils are working individually or in groups.

As collaborative teaching requires so much time, it is important to ensure that it is used effectively, and that both mentors and interns are aware of why they are using it at any given time. It is only useful to help interns develop certain kinds of expertise; for example, speaking to a whole class (exposition or task-setting); chairing a class discussion; question-and-answer; working with slow learners; providing extension activities and working with more able pupils. It would therefore be inappropriate to use it if the intern's main concern at that time was with developing techniques of classroom management, since the need is to work with the whole class on their own to assess how well they are achieving their objectives. It is helpful to identify with interns what kind of skills they are most keen to work on, and, to some extent, plan the lesson around these to allow them the opportunities they need.

In the early stages of training, collaborative teaching is most useful for allowing the intern to focus on certain basic techniques, but later on it can still serve a very valuable function by extending the range of activities which an intern feels able to tackle, or by encouraging him or her to be more flexible. A science mentor, for example, found collaborative teaching a useful way of allowing an intern to explore the issue of differentiated learning (the setting of tasks appropriate to pupils of different abilities). By teaching a practical lesson with her mentor, the intern was able to gain the confidence and practical experience she needed to set up a range of different experiments.

## CONCLUSIONS

Collaborative teaching can obviously only provide one small element within a teacher training programme. It demands a lot of time, and is only suited to the practice of certain aspects of classroom teaching. However it has an extremely useful role to play, especially in the early stages of training, in allowing interns to come to terms with real teaching, while remaining in a protected environment. It enables interns to practise specific teaching skills without requiring them to take on the whole complex process of teaching at once. By removing some of the panic and confusion, it allows interns to approach the task of teaching much more rationally, both while engaged in teaching, and in analysing it afterwards.

Planning with a mentor not only gives the intern access to an experienced teacher's insights and understanding about how to approach a particular class or subject, it also impresses upon the intern the need for rigorous planning. Joint planning is of course also useful to the mentor as a means of exploring the intern's ideas and level of thinking. This can help the mentor in working out how much the intern has learned about teaching, and how best to support the process of learning. Collaborative lessons, while hard work, have generally proved to be enjoyable and stimulating for intern, mentor and pupils. They have also often been a source of great new teaching ideas!

## REFERENCES

1. For an explanation of both the underlying principles, and the practical organisation of the Internship Scheme see Benton, P. (ed.). (1990). *The Oxford Internship Scheme*. Calouste Gulbenkian Foundation.
2. This data was collected as part of the OUDES DeMMent Project (Develop-

ment of Materials for Mentor Training). This is a research and development project that began in September 1990.

3. 'Craft Knowledge' is used here to mean the sophisticated knowledge and understanding that underlies the classroom practice of experienced teachers. The term is taken from research work by Donald McIntyre and Sally Brown for the Scottish Education Department 1984–8; see especially Brown, S. and McIntyre, D., 'The Professional Craft Knowledge of Teachers', *Scottish Educational Review* (1988), special issue entitled *The Quality of Teaching* edited by Gatherer, W.A. For an analysis of one way in which beginning teachers can gain access to this knowledge through discussion of an observed lesson see McAlpine, A., Brown, S., McIntyre, D., and Hagger, H. (1988). *Student-teachers Learning from Experienced Teachers*. SCRE Project Report, Edinburgh.

4. See McIntyre, D., 'Ideas and Principles Guiding the Internship Scheme', in Benton, P. (ed.). (1990). *The Oxford Internship Scheme*. Calouste Gulbenkian Foundation.

## Chapter 10

# Peer Support as the Basis of Good Mentoring Practice

Barry Featherstone and Steve Smith

This is an account of how the establishment of a Learning Support Team (LST) led to the development of a group of teachers who can offer mentoring support to any colleague in the school. Although the initial creation of the team was a response to a powerful series of coincidences, its activities have subsequently demonstrated that in-house mutual mentoring has significant and positive consequences for the professional development of staff. This must, in turn, be of benefit to the pupils.

## THE CLIMATE FOR CHANGE

In describing the 'coming together' of the various factors which resulted in the creation of the Learning Support Team at Deacon's it is important to recognise that the series of coincident events which produced, even demanded, this development are unlikely to be reproduced in other contexts. The LST was the 'big idea', the solution to a number of complex difficulties encountered by this particular school.

But it is also important to view the development of the LST as a fundamental change of attitude as much as a response to problems. School-wide commitment to the enhancement of classroom practice through the development of positive mentor relationships, such as was generated before the introduction of the LST, is not dependent on any given context. It is this climate of opinion which is so vital – a prerequisite even – for the success of any move towards a 'mentoring school'. This climate must be actively pursued through an analysis of the structures, systems and attitudes which prevail in a school if the creation of a similar team is to have any chance of success.

What follows is an account of the various circumstances in which

Deacon's became involved in a network of peer support involving a large number of staff. There is a danger of over-simplifying, and even of understating the impact of some of these circumstances relative to others by implying they were of equal importance. Retrospectively, some influences were more powerful than others, but no attempt is made to distinguish between them here.

The school had seen a year of rapid change in 1989. The arrival of a new head and the establishment of a new senior management team was a catalyst for significant and rapid development. Among many crucial changes was the creation of a Senior Council and a comprehensive meetings structure which allowed proper discussion of ideas to occur. Over the two previous years the school intake had changed considerably. With a 40 per cent ESL (English as a Second Language) intake Section XI staff had been appointed to the school. The Special Needs Co-ordinator identified a 10 per cent increase in pupils with learning difficulties. Resources were stretched to the limit. There had also been a significant move away from rigid setting policies towards mixed ability groups, and the adoption of a comprehensive 'Education For All' policy concerned with generating the conditions in which all students genuinely enjoyed equal access to the curriculum.

INSET also produced increasing demands on staff time in 1989. Very few weeks passed without the absence of at least one member of staff and the employment of supply. It was time to review the nature of INSET provision and to look for a less disruptive model. It is interesting to note that at the same time the DES (1990) suggested to all school managers that they look for ways to allow for staff training that could be organised to create the minimum disruption to the work of the school. It was also recognised that there was among the staff the expertise needed to cover most INSET demands without colleagues going out of the school.

These factors still might not have been sufficient to drive the necessary changes. There were, however, others. It became apparent fairly early in the year that at least one member of staff new to the school was struggling. A programme of in-class 'mentor' support was quickly put in place (initially as a damage limitation exercise) and it soon became clear that a considerable improvement in performance was being achieved. This 'solution' was relatively expensive (additional staffing being bought in to provide the support) and there were obvious concerns about the outcome in the longer term, as costs became prohibitive. These fears, though, proved unfounded as the steady improvement continued even as the support was slowly withdrawn.

As the academic year progressed the publication of the Elton Report, with its clear messages about peer support, seemed to reinforce beliefs held within the school. The appointment of three probationers, a licensed teacher and a number of other 'trainees' (returners and an instructor) brought the need for a comprehensive policy of mentoring into even sharper focus. It became widely accepted that all staff had an entitlement to such support. Indeed it was recognised that in this period of rapid change it was in fact the more experienced staff who were having the greater difficulty in adapting their teaching styles to meet the needs of their mixed ability classes and the demands of the National Curriculum.

Perhaps the final element fell into place through the production of the School Development Plan. As part of the process all staff were consulted about priorities in terms of (i) whole-school, (ii) the various groups (departments, pastoral teams) within the school and (iii) individual needs. The degree of consensus was extraordinary. The need for the development of teaching and learning styles was a high priority in responses at all levels.

## THE LEARNING SUPPORT TEAM

By the end of 1989 it was widely recognised that a significant reorganisation of the Special Needs and Section XI staff would be needed to produce a co-ordinated Learning Support Team.

This LST was to be managed by a senior member of staff who was also a head of faculty. The team also had a Co-ordinator for Special Needs and for Section XI – both on Scale B. They were both full-time members of the team off-timetable. The full-time team was increased by two full-time Section XI teachers, and heads of department in maths, English and science were allocated at least one period per week to work with the team. Learning support assistants and a bilingual assistant made up the full team.

The task of the LST was to provide support across the curriculum for all pupils identified as having learning or language difficulties. Through this brief it was expected that the LST would work with the classroom teacher. The teaching staff were expected to work co-operatively with their subject counterparts. Learning support and bilingual assistants would be principally involved with pupil support.

The LST met weekly to discuss issues relating to pupil difficulties and strategies required to overcome them. In the early stages the team recognised that they would never be able to provide sufficient individual support. Their main input needed to be towards supporting the teacher and developing teaching styles which would make the curriculum more accessible to all pupils. Departments were asked to assess their need and identify an action plan for staff development. The LST, with its flexible timetable, would respond to these needs. In some cases this involved one member of the LST working with one subject teacher for a concentrated period of time (eg one term). Elsewhere it allowed for the release of department staff to observe colleagues in the classroom.

Predominantly the support requested was collaborative teaching with certain year groups, as schemes of work and teaching styles were developed. For this, liaison time had to be created so that the participants could plan and evaluate on a regular basis. The LST members were not experts overnight. Some attended courses on collaborative teaching. All attended regular departmental meetings. The deputy head ran a training session in mentoring skills for both members of the LST and heads of departments.

The model which emerged then was radically different from one directed purely at pupil support. Rather it provided flexible mentoring for all staff who requested it as they strove to widen their repertoire of teaching styles. In addition, on those occasions when external INSET was essential, then the LST staff could provide continuity and more effective cover than any supply staff.

As a concept, the LST seemed to be very much in tune with current thinking and with the best in current practice. Clearly the role of Special Needs departments in secondary school has changed dramatically in a short time. It was only in 1984 that the DES was advocating the need for the influence of Special Needs staff to be 'permeating the whole school'. It suggested that there was a need for improvement in 'the provision and organisation of . . . co-operative working by staff as a team' (1984, p. 45). Gulliford (1985, pp. 43–4) observed that 'A wider role for the remedial teacher had been developing, as an adviser to other staff, sometimes involving assistance and co-teaching in the ordinary classroom.' Just six years later the in-support role of the Special Needs teacher is common in most secondary schools. Having moved away from the deficit model of remedial teaching, Special Needs teachers now see themselves as agents of change in the mainstream classrooms, and the notion of in-class support has become the norm. It is the nature of this support and the role of the change agent that are now crucial. Swann (1988) advocates a more positive role for the support teacher – a role which is firmly based on the intention to help colleagues develop their range of teaching and learning styles:

It may be more useful to think of the curriculum, not as knowledge to be conveyed, but as a set of teaching and learning relationships by which that knowledge is conveyed. And it may be more useful to think of the job of support teaching as improving the quality of those relationships. (p. 98)

But the in-class support model is not merely the means for developing curriculum access for all pupils. It is also a basis for staff development through peer support. It was the school's stated philosophy that all teachers were teachers of Special Needs and therefore responsible for the learning of all pupils in their class, and it was recognised that the classroom teacher would need support in meeting those needs. The LST established that members of the team would work with the teachers by supporting them with the whole class. Both teachers would be responsible for all the pupils within the class, working together to provide curriculum access for them all.

It was expected that this exercise of collaborative teaching would be of benefit to both teachers, as it provided a possible solution to one of the most intractable problems associated with developments in class-room practice. Any change in teaching practices can be threatening for many teachers. They may feel isolated and de-skilled. Even when a teacher has followed a course which develops the theory and even demonstrates the practice, he or she often does not have the confidence to experiment in the classroom. When a working relationship has been developed between the LST teacher and the subject teacher, the development of alternative styles of teaching and managing learning can take place in the security of mutual support.

## MANAGING THE INNOVATION

Such a radical change in organisation of Special Needs and ESL provision needed careful and tactful management as well as the full support of the senior management team. The rationale was clearly spelt out to all staff. It was also agreed that in the early stages LST staff would only work with colleagues who specifically requested support. Materials support and guidance with individual programmes of study would continue. In the first term, there were enough volunteers to occupy the LST fully. Senior management showed their support by allowing a timetabled liaison period between class teachers and LST staff. This permitted a working dialogue to develop between the two parties. The presence of a second adult in the classroom can be threatening for many secondary teachers and the first half term during which two colleagues are developing a working relationship requires tactful management. It is therefore essential that the two teachers concerned have a chance to build up and firmly establish this relationship that is based on mutual trust. It is a period when the two participants will work in collaboration, sharing the teaching, preparation and marking. Only when this relationship is well established can any form of staff development be considered. Then is the time for the two teachers to begin to discuss development of classroom practice.

Lewis (1984) questioned whether Special Needs teachers were adequately prepared to teach across the curriculum. In fact the need for the support teacher to discuss the content and depend on the subject specialist for advice on the content of the lesson is a key feature which sets the stage for the development of mutual interdependence. The subject teacher has control of the content. This begins the debate. Issues relating to presentation of lessons, planning and teaching style arise naturally from the content. The support teacher becomes dependent on the subject teacher for specialist content knowledge. The specialist therefore maintains his or her self-esteem and so is more open to listening to ideas about developing ways of teaching that content. When there is a receptiveness to change, a willingness to experiment and an openness to express reservations and worries, then the partnership teaching can begin and the staff development will follow.

## THEORY INTO PRACTICE: AN EXAMPLE

The best illustration of this process is provided by a brief account of how this policy was implemented with considerable success in one particular curriculum area over a period of two terms. The account is kept deliberately vague in order to protect the confidentiality guaranteed to the participants. In this particular case the department had identified a need to develop materials and teaching styles for pupils with learning difficulties. Each member of the LST had been allocated a faculty area with which to work. The LST member allocated to the department was experienced in Special Needs and had had recent class teaching experience. The class teacher was an experienced member of staff. The class was a Year 7 group of 25, containing three pupils with learning difficulties and two with language difficulties. The group had three lessons per week. The support teacher arranged to support in all these lessons and a liaison period was established. In the first half term the support teacher concentrated on the five pupils with difficulties. The liaison period allowed a discussion about the materials to be used and some of the problems they were causing. The support teacher's input was concerned with adapting the materials for the pupils with language/learning difficulties. The lesson format followed a regular pattern. First there was a brief oral introduction to the topic, after which worksheets were distributed and pupils worked individually on the task. The classroom was arranged in groups of four, though there were no group activities. The teachers were then fully occupied in responding to pupils' frequent requests for help and general supervision to ensure they remained on task.

It was apparent to the support teacher that many children were finding the work too difficult. At the same time both teachers recognised a deterioration in behaviour and motivation. Initially the class teacher enlisted the help of the support teacher in adapting materials to provide some differentiation. This opened the dialogue on teaching and learning styles. Although the differentiated materials allowed for more successful completion of tasks, there was still little enthusiasm and the only apparent interest shown by the pupils was the completion of the task as quickly as possible. The support teacher had, by this time, become involved in the initial introduction to the lesson with similar limited outcomes. This brought about the first positive discussions about changing classroom practice. The class teacher and support teacher had now had the common experience of less than successful practice.

In the early stages of introducing change the class teacher stayed on the periphery, leaving the support teacher to conduct the lessons. As the class responded with enthusiasm to the newly devised activities she gradually became more involved to the point where she asked to lead a later group activity before she was due to take over. As the activities became more varied the need for the support teacher to 'target' those pupils with language/learning difficulties diminished. In the early stages, with the class teacher again leading the sessions, the liaison periods became more an opportunity for reflection on what had succeeded, what had failed and why. The support teacher was there to offer encouragement and recognise success. Failings were openly discussed and suggestions shared. As the term progressed the class teacher was happy for the support teacher to withdraw.

This account simplifies the actual events to the point where they may appear easy to achieve. In evaluating the process, however, it is vital to identify the ingredients which brought about this success in turning theory into actual practice. First there had to be the flexibility of LST time so that the support teacher could respond to need and adjust time availability accordingly. Second, there had to be careful development of the relationships leading to mutual trust between class and support teachers. Third, the support teacher needed to have the confidence to teach in a non-specialist area and the expertise and experience to carry this off effectively. Above all, though, the class teacher had to have the willingness to learn, the commitment to change and the courage to persevere when faced with the difficult realities of the situation. There were inevitable setbacks. There is no gain without pain.

# RESOURCING

If the reader is encouraged to contemplate a similar venture then the cost of such an arrangement must also be considered. Unlike the traditional model of INSET where the costs of a course, the supply staff, the travel and subsistence can easily be identified and wholly attributed to a particular piece of staff development, the LST model is altogether more complex. The straightforward calculation of a cost per lesson presents few difficulties, but what proportion of this cost can be seen as pupil support and what as staff development?

Clearly whenever two teachers are present in the same classroom they both make a contribution to the learning environment and this makes the notion of 'costing' the staff development rather subjective, perhaps even arbitrary. The example outlined above represents a fairly typical level of input needed to achieve a significant development in teaching and learning style. At current Deacon's staffing costs the necessary four periods per week of support over two terms would represent an investment of over £1800. What proportion of this should be seen as INSET and what as pupil support should probably be left to accountants, and whether this investment represents good value for money is a matter for individual judgement and opinion.

What is not in dispute among those involved is that it is difficult to conceive of any 'extraction' model of INSET being as effective as peer support was. How the initiative as a whole has been funded needs to be viewed in the context in which it developed. This reinforces the point made several times earlier that whole systems cannot be lifted from one institution and simply 'transplanted' into another. The finance was created at Deacon's by the integration of Special Needs staffing with Section XI posts, and by topping up with money from the TVEI and school INSET budgets. It is also true to say that in the first year of operation the cost of staffing for the curriculum included a major element of what we describe as 'Curriculum Support Time'. That is, certain key members of staff were given remission from timetabled lessons in order that they might make a significant contribution to the LST. This 'enhancement' model is well established at Deacon's and represents one way in which LMS can be exploited to deliver what the school judges to be a priority.

Perhaps any comparison of costs between various models of staff development ought to start with their effectiveness. If an exercise in staff development fails to improve and enrich the learning of the children it can never be thought of as 'value for money', however low the cost. This raises the whole debate as to the purpose of INSET and a teacher's entitlement to training for individual reasons rather than for the needs of the institution. This is obviously beyond the scope of this chapter, but is an issue which must be raised with staff before INSET budgets are spent in alternative ways. Such a discussion is part of the process of establishing the right climate for the establishment of an LST, for if it is not confronted at the start of the process it is likely to surface during it! Initiating the debate is the only honest management strategy. If the argument cannot be won within an individual school the LST concept may not be an appropriate way forward.

## TOWARDS A MENTORING SCHOOL

The success of the LST in their dual role of pupil support and staff development is in no small measure due to the fact that at Deacon's we were fortunate to have a team which contained staff who were experienced classroom teachers with additional expertise in Special Needs and ESL. The evolution of the staff development role would have been even smoother had it been directed solely towards probationers and other less experienced staff members. Yet the very fact that the more ambitious position (that of seeing peer support as an entitlement for all) was taken, served to give the concept real credibility.

Moreover, it was never the intention to give sole responsibility for the many 'official' trainees in the school to the LST. There was an important need at the time to develop the role and the skills of many of the heads of department and teachers in charge of subjects within the school. The solution seemed to be to assign each of the 'trainees' a departmental mentor and have their activities co-ordinated by the 'professional tutor'. During the 1990–91 academic year, then, seven fairly experienced members of the staff were acting in the mentor capacity to one trainee each.[1] During the year a limited amount of training was offered to these and future (potential) mentors in areas such as lesson observation skills and debriefing interviews, but in truth this is a key area for future development if our vision of a mentoring school is to be achieved.

In the past when one thought of 'mentoring' it conjured up images of a senior member of staff, probably a deputy, supervising a probationer or student. This may have involved the occasional visit to the classroom followed by a friendly chat over coffee in which ideas were exchanged about improving the performance of the trainee. There may also have

---

[1] 'Trainees' during the year included 3 probationers, 1 licensed teacher, 2 instructors appointed to shortage subject areas and 2 teachers returning to the profession involved in a job-share arrangement. As the year progressed 3 students who came to join the staff were also mentored in this way, making a total of 11.

been informal discussions with departmental heads and other col-leagues in the pastoral teams. The reports on progress were almost always written by the deputy concerned. How much real training can be thought to have been achieved – indeed how much ought to be expected? As the Licensed and Articled Teacher Schemes, and other initiatives such as external PGCEs clearly demonstrate, schools have a major role in providing training for a whole range of differently skilled and experienced 'new' entrants. The demands of the National Curricu-lum and other initiatives inevitably mean experienced, trained col-leagues will also need to widen their repertoire of teaching and learning styles.

How much better is it that such 'training' begins with the sharing of ideas at the planning stages, and is followed up by two teachers working together in the same classroom to introduce the change? The success, or otherwise, of the innovation can then be evaluated openly with both parties learning from the experience. Why should such a process be limited to 'trainees'? Many schools recognise that a policy for staff development should embrace all staff throughout their careers and that there are many alternatives to the 'supply'-based model of in-service training. At Deacon's we would argue that mentoring through managed peer support in class is an effective model for such ongoing staff development, and as one of many arms of a co-ordinated policy it has enormous potential. As has been made clear earlier, such an arrangement depends on the establishment of the right atmosphere, that is, a climate where there is mutual trust, respect and confidence. The fact that the time was right for such a development meant that all parties were keen to make it work. It soon became obvious to all, even those not directly involved, that there were far more benefits to having two people in the classroom than were anticipated. The power of this message spreading through the staffroom began to overcome any feelings of insecurity about having a second adult present.

Deacon's has moved from a 'closed' environment to one where what we have come to know as the 'drop in' culture thrives. The demand for peer support now exceeds supply. The LST is now a well-established part of the school ethos and many staff view their mentor role as one to be relished, and an important element in the success of their depart-ment and ultimately therefore of the school. The growing climate of confidence provides an excellent base from which to develop still further the notion of collaborative mentoring to a point where it becomes embedded within the structures of the school to the benefit of staff at all levels. More importantly, of course, this collaboration will continue to improve the quality of teaching and learning thus enriching the experience of our pupils.

## REFERENCES

Dean, J. (1989) *Special Needs in the Secondary School: The Whole School Approach*. Routledge.

DES. (1984). *Slow Learning and Less Successful Pupils in the Secondary School*. DES.

DES. (1989). *Discipline in Schools* (The Elton Report). HMSO.

DES. (1990). *Developing School Management*. DES.

Gulliford, R. (1985). *Teaching Children with Learning Difficulties*. NFER.

Lewis, G. (1984). 'A supportive role at secondary level', *Remedial Education*, vol. 19, (1).

Swann, W. (1988). 'Integration or differentiation' in Thomas, G. and Feiler, A. (Eds). *Planning for Special Needs*. Oxford. Blackwell.

*Chapter 11*

# Structured Mentoring and the Development of Teaching Skill

Mike Berrill

## ON NECESSITY BEING THE MOTHER OF INVENTION

Ours is an 11–16 boys' comprehensive school with 67 per cent ethnic minority pupils. Though over a third of our intake receive free school meals and the Year 7 test results on the NFER-Nelson Cognitive Abilities Test are skewed way below average, by the time our pupils come to sit external exams they consistently achieve national average or above average pass rates. We have very low truancy, little or no vandalism and, in a school with a potential for racial conflict, there is a high level of harmony. Staff absenteeism is low and bears testimony to high levels of staff morale and commitment. In short we are a friendly and successful school community.

When recruiting teachers, however, we recognise that the school is not always an attractive proposition: we are single sex, have no sixth form, are housed in very basic post-war buildings, and serve a catchment area which includes some of the poorest housing stock in Luton. Relatively high house prices play a part and sadly racism in the community is also a factor. Advertisements in the *Times Educational Supplement* will often have a low or nil response. There is no doubt that in recent years we have suffered from the national staffing crisis.

For some time now, when we have been unable to recruit, we have taken mature, experienced adults with an interest in young people (careers officers, youth leaders, church leaders) and have employed them as 'instructors'. With support, many have become effective teachers and we have every reason to be grateful to them. There was always an uneasiness however, about their lack of formal training and a worry that they were in a position to be exploited. When the Licensed Teacher Scheme was announced we therefore welcomed it as a way of offering our instructors the kind of support and training which would enable them to become full members of the profession.

From the beginning, the school developed a set of criteria for any training scheme for use with instructors. So that they should have professional credibility at the end of the licensed period we argued that training should be:

- practical: of direct relevance to the teacher's daily experience;
- coherent: form a thorough, sequenced programme of training;
- rigorous: make intellectual/academic demands equivalent to second or third year undergraduate level;
- externally evaluated: involve assignments/examinations that were marked externally;
- creditable: involve forms of evaluation that carried accreditation or had the potential to do so.

At this stage we made the important decision that we would conduct this training on site. This was based on two strong convictions: first that there existed within the school a wealth of experience on teaching and learning which could be tapped, and second, that expertise which existed elsewhere should properly be drawn in and developed within the school. We were determined that we would develop our own school-based scheme. We studied the licensed teacher training criteria contained in DES circular 18/89 and also the redrafted initial teacher training (ITT) criteria of circular 24/89 (CATE 2). In broad terms we interpreted these as calling for three areas of development:

- subject studies: knowledge and expertise in preferred subject area(s) equivalent to 2nd or 3rd year undergraduate level;
- educational and professional studies: training in knowledge, concepts and values sufficient to ensure initiation into the various dimensions of the professional debate on education;
- subject application: training in the competences and skills associated with effective classroom practice in a particular subject area.

Our initial strategy was to buy in the resources we needed to effect this training and in the first two areas we found a rich source of material at the Open University. Subject studies, where the teacher did not already possess the requisite expertise, could be developed through the OU's Associate Student Programme; basically an opportunity to study the full range of undergraduate units without enrolling on a degree course. All these courses carry full or half credits.

We were also delighted to find that the OU had the equivalent of a secondary PGCE professional studies course in 'Frameworks for Teaching' (Course EP228). The DES paid the OU over a million pounds to develop this course which was primarily designed to allow science and maths graduates to train in non-teacher training institutions. The course provides a thorough and coherent introduction to the major dimensions of the professional debate, is externally evaluated and carries a half credit.

We were less fortunate in our search for resources outside the school to facilitate the development of classroom practice. Though there were materials aimed at developing particular aspects of teaching, we found nothing of a more comprehensive or general nature. None of the books on classroom management was easy to translate into a structured programme for developing teaching skill and we felt that if we wanted to adopt a systematic approach we would have to develop it ourselves. At this stage we had only a vague sense of what such a programme might be like. The one thing which seemed fairly clear was a sense of 'process'. We had already carried out a pilot study, involving 20 staff, on the value of peer observation as a way of developing teaching and learning strategies. The findings of the national pilot project on appraisal confirmed our view that the process of pre-observation discussion, classroom observation, review and target setting was potentially a powerful learning mechanism.

We did not have any clear ideas, however, on what the 'content' behind such a process would be like. At the beginning, we assumed that we were looking for certain 'principles of teaching'; quasi-theoretical descriptions of good practice which would lead to teaching proficiency. We discovered quickly how naïve this hope had been and it came as a surprise. Even though we may have been unable to articulate them, we had assumed that a range of shared technical skills underpinned our practice. As we looked at research on good teaching, however, it seemed to us that this assumption was a myth.

While it has always been possible to identify good teaching by the quality of learning outcomes it produces, actually specifying what effective teachers do and thereby providing ourselves with guidelines for development, has been far more difficult. Years of research have failed to identify even the simplest regularities in effective practice. Good teachers, it seems, achieve their results by using a wide variety of approaches that are rarely transferable to other people or other situations. Clearly there are teaching strategies that should logically promote learning – sequencing of material, progressive revision, feedback of results – but the crucial and yet intangible factor is always judgement. Take a simple strategy like 'giving praise'. In the folklore of teaching it is regarded as almost self-evident that there is a linear relationship between praise given and pupil motivation. As Berliner (1976) remarks, however:

> We have seen positive verbal reinforcement used with a new child in the class, one who was trying to win peer-group acceptance, and whose behaviour the teacher chose to use as a standard of excellence. We watched silently as the class rejected the intruder, while the teacher's count in the verbal praise category went up and up and up (p. 372).

In short, there is no 'right way' to teach: there are no simple pathways to teaching excellence.

Toms sums this up well when he says:

> Once teaching phenomena are recognised as being man-made and teaching problems are viewed as having multiple potential solutions whose effectiveness is largely unknown prior to the act of teaching, the potential of teacher effectiveness knowledge is dramatically reduced (Dale, 1988 p. 49).

This came as a serious blow to our project since the 'content' of our framework had disappeared.

We decided at this stage to go back to the 'process' and examine how it worked, to see what ideas it might call for. This led us to reflect upon exactly what it is we do when we go in to observe a colleague's professional practice. We realised that, in the initial stages, we may not observe the teacher at all. We often begin by looking at the pupils and, more or less consciously, ask simple questions such as:

- are they behaving positively towards
  - the teacher?
  - other pupils?
  - their work?
- are they 'on task' and engaged in their learning?
- are they paying attention when necessary?
- do they look relaxed and self-confident?
- are they working independently of the teacher?

To a very large extent, if the answer to these questions is 'Yes', then whatever that teacher is doing is good practice. It is only when the answer to some of them is, 'No', that we begin to hypothesise about what may be going wrong and how we may put it right. This gave us our first clue as to what was needed: a framework of ideas from which we could generate practical hypotheses; a pool of 'maybes':

- maybe the teacher does not have clear ground rules?
- maybe the 'task setting' is not clear?
- maybe the voice could be firmer and more expressive?

It was not necessary for this framework to be exhaustive; it simply needed to be a source of practical ideas. We set ourselves the task, through reading, discussion and reflection, of generating this pool of ideas and soon it numbered over a hundred items ranging from providing 'bright, well-ventilated teaching areas' and 'efficient resource distribution' to 'setting clear standards for pupil work' and 'providing positive feedback on performance'. It became clear that for the sake of convenience, if nothing else, these would need to be grouped into different areas of practice, and it is here that we introduced the idea of a 'competence'.

For our purposes we defined a competence as an element of a skill that can be identified and practised separately. It is a useful concept in this context as its ordinary language meaning implies adequacy with regard to certain performance criteria without necessarily signalling broader expertise. Using it we were able to group the practical ideas into what we loosely termed 'competence areas'. The categories that emerged had no ontological status; they were merely convenient groupings for what would otherwise have been an unwieldy list of ideas.

## A FOUNDATION FOR EXCELLENCE

It was in this way that the mentoring framework began to grow around the idea of 'competence areas' made up of clusters of practical ideas, and we began to put our own mentoring handbook together. Twelve competences emerged from this (see Figure 11.1). In building this framework, great effort went into creating independent categories where proficiency in one area was not necessarily associated with proficiency in another. This is well illustrated in what we have called the 'Relationship Competences'. It is entirely possible to have good 'classroom control' yet poor 'teaching performance' and poor 'rapport with pupils' (I remember such teachers only too well from my own childhood!); similar patterns are found with each of the other competences.

In all, there are over 200 practical ideas grouped into competence areas in the mentoring handbook and each is formulated as a question to be examined wherever possible in an observed lesson. By way of example, Figure 11.2 shows the practical criteria associated with competence area 1: 'Use of planning framework'. These criteria are not

**Figure 11.1** *Competence areas*

| | |
|---|---|
| 1. Use of planning framework | PREPARATORY |
| 2. Environment for learning | AREAS |
| 3. Resource development and management | |
| 4. Classroom control | RELATIONSHIP |
| 5. Teaching performance | AREAS |
| 6. Rapport with pupils | |
| 7. Lesson organisation | MANAGEMENT OF |
| 8. Promotion of learning | LEARNING |
| 9. Flexibility | AREAS |
| 10. Subject competence | PROFESSIONAL |
| 11. Pastoral competence | AREAS |
| 12. Professional approach | |

**Figure 11.2** *Criteria for 'Use of planning framework'*

Does the observed lesson show:

- relevance to a syllabus*?
- continuity and progression within a scheme of work*?
- relevance to a stated lesson plan?
- clarity of expected outcomes regarding:

  - knowledge
  - concepts
  - skills            } to be learned?
  - values

- content, method, structure appropriate to intended outcomes?
- incorporation of cross-curricular themes*?
- adequate differentiation for range of ability*?

* Indicates head of department responsibility, and the possible need for separate institutional development. See also text.

exhaustive, and together the teacher and mentor are encouraged to add others. Not all of them reflect on the competence of the trainee. For example, the existence of relevant syllabuses and schemes of work will reflect on the head of department. This fact is acknowledged both in Figure 11.2 and in the handbook by the use of an asterisk (where * above) next to relevant items and indicates where separate institutional development may be necessary.

The basic layout of the handbook began to take shape, but before we could continue we had to sort out a theoretical problem. If good teaching as not the straightforward application of standard techniques, what was it? It seemed to us that the great complexity of the teaching/learning process seems pointed to three levels of skill development:

1. A practical awareness of the various 'competences' associated with effective teaching and basic proficiency in each of them.
2. The gradual integration of these competences into a skilled teaching repertoire.
3. The flexible deployment of appropriate parts of this repertoire according to skilled judgements about the requirements of the learning situation.

If this were the case, then in the initial stages it was important that the main focus of activity should be the systematic development of the separate competence areas. At later stages mentoring activity could

**Figure 11.3**   *Criteria for 'Environment for learning'*

---

Level 1:   Not Evident
Awareness of the criteria associated with this competence is not yet evident or evident only in a rudimentary way:
- basically clean room but littered, untidy, no display.

Level 2:   Elementary
There is some awareness of the criteria associated with this competence and several are receiving elementary attention:
- room tidy, no litter, simple posters.

Level 3:   Growing Competence
There is evidence of a developed understanding of the criteria and over half have been met:
- tidy, simple posters, some pupils' work displayed, form notice board.

Level 4:   Basic Proficiency
There is evidence that this area is well understood; most of the criteria have been met and basic proficiency has been achieved:
- clean, well kept, good desk layout, attractive, regularly changed posters and children's work, up-to-date notice board.

Level 5:   Well Developed
This competence area is being managed with awareness, understanding and confidence:
- colourful and attractive room with stimulating, well-mounted, regularly changed display work, well laid out with readily available resource material; artefacts and plants.

---

focus more on the issue of 'judgement'. It was this insight that brought the whole project together.

Through mentoring we could concentrate our early efforts on ensuring that the separate competences which form the foundation of a successful teaching career are clearly identified and developed to an acceptable level of proficiency. Accordingly the final element in our mentoring framework was a simple five-stage assessment scheme which the mentor could use to indicate when basic proficiency had been reached in a particular competence area. Although the number of levels was arbitrary, five allowed for sufficient discrimination without making assessment over-complicated. The assessment scheme is given in Figure 11.3 with examples of the observations you might expect to find at each level if you were focusing on competence area 2: 'Environment for Learning'.

By now we had decided to use the framework with probationary teachers and we decided that to be recommended for full QTS a licensed teacher or probationer should reach level 4 (basic proficiency) in all 12 competence areas.

## THE FORMATIVE PROCESS

Building on the ideas we had developed, the formative process now became straightforward. It is as follows:

1. Once every three weeks the mentor and trainee together choose a competence area for focus and designate a particular lesson in which the various criteria will be incorporated and explored.
2. In a pre-observation meeting each of the criteria to be considered is discussed, to explore:
   - what they mean;
   - how they might relate to or be incorporated within a lesson;
   - what the teacher will have to do prior to the lesson in terms of planning/development.
   (The 12 competences are in no particular sequence and can be taken in any order depending on the teacher's needs at the time. Experience suggests that 1, 4, 7 and 8 are important early on.)
3. Agreement is reached on which criteria are to be used as a basis for observation in the designated lesson. (It may be that the mentor and teacher decide not to focus on particular criteria for the first few observations but see what issues arise.)
4. In a post-observation meeting the mentor should feedback to the teacher what was observed. This should form the basis for a discussion and a negotiated assessment of:

(a) which criteria have been satisfactorily fulfilled;

(b) which 'level' has been reached in that particular competence area.

(Though specific criteria may be under focus, this should not prevent the discussion widening to consider other features of the lesson worthy of comment. The most important function of this meeting, however, is target-setting, where realistic development tasks are set for the coming weeks and are recorded on the relevant pro forma in the handbook.)

5. Three weeks later the teacher and mentor repeat the process but choosing other competence areas. At the end a formative assessment is made but consideration is also given to targets set from previous months. Any improvement is recorded and dated and the assessment level revised accordingly.

6. The process continues until all twelve competences have received individual focus and a cumulative profile is developed.

The handbook also contains guidelines on how the teacher/mentor relationship should develop if it is to be productive. The point is made strongly that it is not an expert/beginner relationship but essentially one between two fellow travellers where one, by virtue of greater experience, has agreed to act as professional guardian, counsellor and friend to another. In addition there are guidelines on the tasks associated with each of the three different stages in the process: pre-observation; observation; and review and target setting.

## STRUCTURED MENTORING IN ACTION

We started using the handbook in the autumn term of 1990 with 18 staff at the school: three licensed teachers, six probationers and their respective mentors. Immediately it created a powerful effect as it provided a basis for practical reflection and professional dialogue on classroom practice: in effect it provided a 'language of teaching'. I acted as mentor to a licensed teacher during the first year, and through the successive cycles of the formative process I watched his level of technical awareness and competence grow. I also witnessed his growing self-confidence and the steady development of his professional judgement. From a personal point of view, after 15 years in the profession, I also experienced a tremendous growth in my own professional understanding and a significant improvement in my classroom practice.

In the spring term of 1991 we invited an LEA field officer into the school to carry out an interim evaluation of the scheme. This took the form of a questionnaire presented to the 18 staff using the mentoring

**Figure 11.4**  *The evaluation questionnaire*

| Questions | No | Undecided | Fairly | Very |
|---|---|---|---|---|
| 1. Do you find the competence areas useful in describing the basic components of teaching? | 0 | 1 | 6 | 11 |
| 2. Have you found the associated criteria useful in understanding these competences? | 1 | 0 | 7 | 10 |
| 3. In practice have you found these criteria useful as points of focus in observed lessons? | 0 | 3 | 6 | 9 |
| 4. In practice has it been straightforward to assess when these criteria have been met (ie when the teacher knows, understands and can demonstrate them)? | 0 | 4 | 12 | 2 |
| 5. Were the pre-observation guidelines useful in structuring pre-observation discussion? | 2 | 1 | 7 | 8 |
| 6. In practice were the tasks associated with pre-observation completed well? | 0 | 2 | 12 | 4 |
| 7. Have you found that criterion-based observation has helped development? | 1 | 4 | 4 | 8 |
| 8. Did you find the observation sheet helped in noting sufficient detail of the lesson to provide a sound basis for feedback and follow-up? | 1 | 7 | 6 | 2 |
| 9. Were the guidelines for follow-up discussion clear and helpful? | 0 | 3 | 12 | 3 |
| 10. Were the achievement levels useful in giving feedback on the degree of proficiency reached? | 1 | 4 | 7 | 5 |
| 11. Was completing the review and target-setting sheet valuable? | 1 | 3 | 4 | 6 |
| 12. Do you find the concept of a teaching profile helpful? | 1 | 2 | 9 | 6 |
| 13. Overall have you found the scheme helpful in developing basic teaching proficiency? | 0 | 5 | 3 | 9 |

handbook, with a follow-up interview for those who volunteered. Figure 11.4 shows the questions and an indication of the responses from the questionnaire (some respondents did not answer all the questions).

Respondents could tick one of four categories: no, undecided, fairly, very. In general, responses were very favourable, bearing in mind that the scheme had been in operation for such a short time and that the handbook had been freestanding and used without any introductory training. It was clear, however, that several improvements were called for:

- The sheet provided in the handbook for recording lesson observation notes was poorly designed and this was given a new layout and enlarged.
- Originally the wording of the assessment levels had been too vague and these were redrafted.
- The review and target-setting sheets were unwieldy and were completely redesigned.

The follow-up interview yielded valuable supplementary information which led to further important improvements:

- Protected mentor periods were put into the timetable and regarded as sacrosanct.
- Two extra areas were added to the framework (subject competence and pastoral competence).
- The principle of timetabling licensed teachers and probationers with different groups that followed the same course was adopted. (This reduces the amount of preparation and increases the extent to which teachers can reflect and adapt.)

The overwhelming message, however, was that the framework was valuable, helpful and it worked. Since then the handbook has been adopted by Bedfordshire LEA for use with all its licensed teachers and it has formed the basis for the County's mentor training programme which forms a certificate course accredited via Bedford College with the CNAA.

## SOME REFLECTIONS

The foregoing is an account of a fairly simple and straightforward piece of institutional development and there are several issues arising from it which we should consider:

1. *The limitations of 'observation' as a means of determining what underlying processes are at work in a classroom.*

The great complexity of the teaching and learning situation is such that it is not always possible to say why a particular lesson went well or badly. The observer may focus on highly visible yet relatively unimportant features of a lesson; perhaps key factors in the classroom dynamic may lie in previous lessons. This fact leads us to suggest that observation is always a creative exercise in hypothesis-making rather than a simple act of 'giving feedback'.

*2. The tensions surrounding the issue of teacher assessment.*

If, as we have suggested, successful teaching involves a combination of technical competence and professional judgement, then the 'assessment' of teachers raises serious problems. While technical competence can be developed and assessed formatively in the way we have described, overall teaching 'skill' can only be assessed by reference to longer term pupil-learning outcomes. Evaluating these outcomes in relation to teacher input is a far more intuitive and tenuous affair than those engaged in 'objective testing' would care to admit. Indeed many teachers would argue that for all practical purposes it is impossible. A problem therefore arises in any competence-based scheme which leads to summative forms of assessment, since technical proficiency does not necessarily equate with teaching excellence. We can say with confidence, however, that teaching excellence involves high levels of proficiency in the competences we have identified.

*3. An outline of the main features of the role of the mentor.*

A description of the mentor as 'professional guardian, counsellor and friend' was mentioned above but clearly this needs to be developed if mentoring is to be adequately conceptualised and taken seriously as a professional activity. Already we are using the six categories of counselling intervention (Heron, 1986) as a model for the various dimensions of mentoring activity:

prescriptive  – telling people what they should do
informative  – providing key knowledge and information
supportive  – affirming an individual's worth
cathartic  – sensitively drawing out and dealing with emotions
confronting  – assertively challenging false or limiting ideas
catalytic  – empowering, by providing the means of independent development

This framework of categories holds out great promise as a means of theorising the practice of mentoring.

*4. The institutional effects of mentoring activity.*

Mentors often confide with some embarrassment a belief that they are deriving more from their mentoring activity than the trainees and there is no doubt that observing the growing competence of a colleague has a corresponding training effect for the mentor. If this effect is multiplied within an institution and the mentors are networked in some way it has the potential for powerful institutional development. It is just such principles which lie behind the concept of total quality management. There is no doubt that in our school it is slowly enhancing our professional ethos. We now have a common language on teaching and learning and we are motivated to engage in discourse by a need to solve real problems that arise during the mentoring process. This is reason enough to incorporate mentoring activity into any new appraisal structures within schools.

All these issues are worth lengthy consideration but I should like instead to use the remaining space to consider the implications of our experiences for the partnership between schools and training institutions. What began for us as an experiment – a straightforward attempt to give our instructors a credible way into the profession – has led us to reflect in some depth upon why this particular approach to developing classroom practice – for both teacher and mentor – should work. Quite quickly we were drawn to the ideas of Donald Schon, especially those found in his book *Educating the Reflective Practitioner* (1991). His stark thesis is laid out in the opening paragraph of the book:

> *The Crisis of Confidence in Professional Knowledge*
> In the varied topography of professional practice, there is a high, hard ground overlooking a swamp. On the high ground, manageable problems lend themselves to solution through the application of research-based theory and technique. In the swampy lowland, messy, confusing problems defy technical solution. The irony of this situation is that the problems of the high ground tend to be relatively unimportant to individuals or society at large, however great their technical interest may be, while in the swamp lie the problems of greatest human concern. The practitioner must choose. Shall he remain on the high ground where he can solve relatively unimportant problems according to prevailing standards of rigor, or shall he descend to the swamp of important problems and non-rigorous inquiry?

His work is a forceful critique of those forms of professional education which elevate theoretical understanding over practical involvement and see the movement from training into professional activity as nothing more than the translation of theory into practice. To suggest this, Schon argues, is to misunderstand fundamentally the way 'professional artistry' develops. It is a major paradox that in countless acts of competence, judgement and skilful performance so little depends 'on our being able to describe what we know how to do or even to entertain in conscious thought the knowledge our action reveals' (ibid, p. 22).

It is a truism that good teachers often cannot tell why they are good. Their skill is actually in their professional activity, not in their subsequent reflection on it. We 'know' far more than we can ever put into words.

Schon says: 'We learn to execute such complex performances as crawling, walking, juggling or riding a bicycle without being able to give a verbal description even roughly adequate to our actual performance' (ibid, p. 24). He calls this skilled performance: 'knowing-in-action'. 'We reveal it by our spontaneous, skilful execution of the performance; and we are characteristically unable to make it verbally explicit' (ibid, p. 25).

It is nevertheless sometimes possible, by observing and then reflecting on skilled performances, to describe some aspects of this implicit knowing-in-action. These are always 'constructions' however; static, partial, limited descriptions of something which is essentially non-linguistic and dynamic. These 'constructions' are always conjectures which need to be tested against observation of performance either of the self or others.

This approach explained several paradoxes we had experienced during the construction of the handbook:

- our difficulty, even as experienced teachers in making explicit our practice;
- the fact that the more we sought 'rigour' (in relation to research evidence) in our mentoring activity, the less 'relevant' our contribution seemed to become;
- the limitations of classroom observation in penetrating underlying classroom processes.

Above all, Schon's suggestion that descriptions of professional knowing-in-action were always constructions – abstract models of activity – articulated well with our understanding of the conceptual status of 'competences' and their associated 'criteria'. It also began to explain why the mentoring process was important.

When things go wrong. Schon argues, we can react to the error signals in two ways:

## 1. Reflection-on-action

We can think back over what happened in order to determine what aspect of the environment, or our performance within it, contributed to the unexpected or unwanted outcome. By mentally re-running the sequence of situation-action-effect we can rehearse amendments to this sequence to see if any of them seem plausible or work in principle. We can then decide to experiment with these new models of action in future performances. In addition to using our existing store of such models we can consciously seek new ones by observing others who are performing in similar situations, engaging in similar activity and seeking similar effects. During such observations we can relate the perceived patterns of situation-action-effect to our existing repertoire and make amendments or add new ones. Here Schon is describing what he calls 'an enquirer's reflective conversation with his situation'. A mentor engaged in observation and follow-up becomes a powerful catalyst in this learning situation. She or he provides a different perspective, rich supplementary information not available to the teacher (a description of performance) and above all an opportunity for dialogue and a continuous reworking of ideas.

## 2. Reflection-in-action
Alternatively, we may reflect in the midst of action without interrupting it. We may still affect the outcome of the situation in hand, so that 'our thinking serves to reshape what we are doing while we are doing it' (ibid, p. 26). Such reflection is a powerful learning medium, for it telescopes several learning stages into a matter of seconds or minutes. For example:

- recognition of a mismatch between intended outcome and actual outcome;
- a questioning of the assumptions or strategies that might underlie the mismatch;
- hypothesising a new model of situation-action-effect and on the spot experiment;
- feedback of results, which may lead to confirmation, amendment, or abandonment of new models.

This also provides rich material for later reflection-on-action when through dialogue, individuals can re-run and mentally rehearse new performance combinations.

The mentor plays a key role here too; her or his sheer presence as observer increases the probability that certain pre-agreed ideas come into focus and are sustained long enough for reflection-in-action to take place.

These complex concepts of Schon's provided a powerful explanatory model for our mentoring framework. Regular, focused mentoring provides sustained opportunities for both teacher and mentor to gain from the powerful learning effects of reflection-on-action and reflection-in-action. We recognised that it was these twin learning modes fuelling the steady growth of that knowing-in-action which eventually equates with teaching excellence. As a result of these reflections we have come to adopt a different perspective on the 'partnership' between schools and training institutions; one which we feel calls for a change in emphasis.

For as long as I have been in the profession there has been a culture of mistrust between practising teachers and those in ITT, and much of Schon's critique explains why. By divorcing theory from practice when they are inseparable, teachers and trainers have constructed for themselves different life-worlds, each of which partially excludes the other.

Though great progress has been made, especially since the reformulation of the CATE criteria, the debate on partnership is too often restricted to the question of 'improving teacher training'. While schools have always been willing to help with this, their needs are broader and deeper. Ultimately they are concerned with creating secure, just and caring institutions which foster the personal, social and intellectual development of their children. Whereas training institutions see the spin-offs of school-based training, such as mentor development as incidental, schools are coming to see them as major goals to be actively pursued. It is here that training institutions have a major role to play, not only in teacher education but also through the dissemination of their expertise, in improving the whole context of teaching and learing.

Furlong, Hirst and their colleagues have done a great deal to clarify the different levels or dimensions of professional preparation. They distinguish four areas of concern:

- Level (a) direct practice – practical training through direct experience in schools and classrooms;
- Level (b) indirect practice – 'detached' training in practical matters usually conducted in classes or workshops within training institutions;
- Level (c) practical principles – critical study of the principles of practice and their use;
- Level (d) disciplinary theory – critical study of practice and its principles in the light of fundamental theory and research.
  (Furlong et al., 1988, p. 132)

Using these conceptual distinctions they argue that whereas level (a) is best achieved in schools, levels (b), (c) and (d) properly belong to training institutions. In the context of teacher education this seems appropriate but in relation to developing the broader issue of teaching and learning in schools, such arrangements effectively disenfranchise the profession in the sense that they rob it of the means to conceptualise and refine its art. What is desperately needed, as schools create those institutional practices and procedures which underpin total quality management, is for levels (b), (c) and (d) to be developed in schools as well.

This calls for a new concept of partnership. It calls for the development of school-based training, using distanced learning materials with training institutions providing periodic on-site tutorials, assignment tasks and external evaluation in addition to general support and advice. In as much as it offers a core activity around which such partnerships could grow, I commend to you the idea of structured mentoring. It begins with practice and here I would agree with Richard Rorty when he says: 'the way to re-enchant the world, to bring back what religion gave to our forefathers, is to stick to the concrete' (Bernstein (ed.), 1985, p. 173).

Structured mentoring combines a powerful learning process with a framework of practical ideas but leaves open the reciprocal issues of explanation and theoretical justification. These are areas where theoretical work cries out to be done. It is here that the expertise locked into training institutions needs to be released. Hundreds of questions need consideration. Some are very basic – 'in what ways can the classroom environment be made more conducive to learning?' – others are more complex – 'when is it appropriate to use ability groupings to achieve educational objectives?' Only when such questions are part of everyday professional debate will teachers become reflectively aware of the various dimensions of their professional activity and be able to give a rational justification for their practice. This will not happen until the profession plays a full and active part in training its own practitioners.

The last words I will leave to the pragmatist John Dewey:

> We are weak today in ideal matters because intelligence is divorced from aspiration . . . When philosophy shall have co-operated with the force of events and made clear and coherent the meaning of the daily detail, science and emotion will interpenetrate, practice and imagination will embrace. Poetry and religious feeling will be the unforced flowers of life (Dewey, in Bernstein, 1985).

## REFERENCES

Berliner, D. C. (1976). 'A status report on the study of teacher effectiveness', *Journal of Research in Science Teaching*, Vol 13.

Bernstein, R. J. (ed.). (1985). *Habermas and Modernity*. Oxford. Blackwell.

Berrill, M. G. (1991). *Foundation for Excellence: A structured approach to mentoring and the development of basic teaching proficiency*. Luton. Challney Community College Press.

Booth, M., Furlong, V. J., Wilkin, M. (1990). *Partnership in Initial Teacher Training*. Cassell.

Dale, R., Furgusson, R., Robinson, A. (1988). *Frameworks for Teaching*. Hodder and Stoughton.

Furlong, V. J., Hirst, P. H., Pocklington, K., and Miles, S. (1988). *Initial Teacher Training and the Role of the School*. Milton Keynes. Open University Press.

Heron, J. (1986). *Six Category Intervention Analysis* (2nd edn). Human Potential Research Project, University of Surrey, Guildford.

Schon, D. (1991). *Educating the Reflective Practitioner*. Jossey-Bass. (Excerpts quoted with permission.)

## Acknowledgements

I am grateful to my senior management colleagues at Challney and friends outside the school who have read and criticised this paper and to Diane Rogers who has patiently typed and retyped the drafts.

# PART IV   Overview

## Chapter 12

# Mentoring as a Staff Development Activity

Mike Kelly, Tony Beck and John apThomas

The term 'mentor' is being used to describe an increasing range of activities. It is used in student and staff induction programmes, and in the articled and licensed teacher training schemes. More and more are those involved reporting the process to be a powerful and cost-effective way of increasing personal and organisational focus and central to the institution's staff development strategies and plans, rather than merely a way of smoothing new staff entry, or offering tips for getting round bureaucratic procedures. Here we consider its use as a significant element in the staff development and target-setting process for all staff including trainees, in the enhancement of their learning and development within their institutions.

## THE MENTORING APPROACH

Mentoring as a basis for staff or student development is founded on the notion of learning and learning styles. Staff development, whether of experienced or novice staff, has to be about individuals learning, that is, changing their behaviour. Without going into a major discussion of how people learn, it is pertinent to refer briefly to the ideas of Kolb who has developed an experiential learning model. It is a model concerned with the systematic and purposeful development of the whole person; it is the kind of learning which leads to people changing. Self-development is rarely successful without the support of other people. A system of mentoring offers that support by providing individuals with someone who can give feedback, question, share, discuss, challenge, confront and guide one through the learning cycle.

The crucial starting point is concrete experience: a happening, or action. Development often starts with a surprise, puzzlement or shock when something has happened that was unexpected or didn't make sense. When this happens a mentor is someone to go to for help. A problem shared can be a problem halved (if not solved) and the sharing can be a crucial stage in the development process, because stage two in the learning cycle involves thinking about the problem or experience.

Reflection which can involve observation and discussion and the generation and evaluation of alternative ways of doing things enables the individual to gain insight into his or her own practice and explore new ways of performing. The mentor can have a vital role to play in this reflection process by observing, discussing, guiding through example, and by coaching.

Stage three involves connecting experiences to conceptual and theoretical frameworks which help make sense of the experiences. Sound development needs new skills underpinned by a rationale, and supported by an understanding of the principles and concepts of good practice. A mentor will probably be able to help in the process of making those connections by dint of greater experience and his or her own prior development as a reflective practitioner.

The last stage involves active experimentation. New ideas need to be internalised and then incorporated into practice; new ways of working and feeling have to be tried out before the learning is complete. The mentor can facilitate and monitor and give feedback on these new actions and help reinforce the development. If the new ideas do not

**Figure 12.1**   *A learning or developmental cycle*

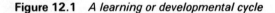

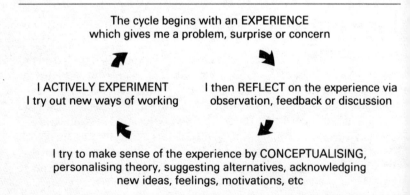

The cycle begins with an EXPERIENCE
which gives me a problem, surprise or concern

I ACTIVELY EXPERIMENT
I try out new ways of working

I then REFLECT on the experience via
observation, feedback or discussion

I try to make sense of the experience by CONCEPTUALISING,
personalising theory, suggesting alternatives, acknowledging
new ideas, feelings, motivations, etc

work, or are only partially successful, then a further problem arises and the cycle starts again (see Figure 12.1).

## HOW IMPORTANT AND USEFUL IS THE MENTORING APPROACH?

There is undoubtedly a tradition of autonomy in the classroom among teachers in British schools, and mentoring does not automatically fit easily into this tradition. However, against this may be seen the growing importance attributed to teamwork and 'pairwork', as organisational and personal strategies for handling:

- some of the responsibilities placed on staff in schools under the Education Reform Act;
- the pressures exerted on schools by the many changes in the social and political expectations and aspirations of the pupils and their parents in the 1990s;
- the increasing levels of negative stress reported to be arising from such a period of rapid change.

Working with a mentor system in some of the ways, and with some of the activities outlined below, can be effective in meeting such challenges in a developmental and personally rewarding way, while at the same time ensuring that the organisation as a whole calls on its stored expertise and experience in meeting its needs and priorities.

## INDUCTION MENTORING: THE NEW HEAD, THE NEW TEACHER, AND THE TRAINEE TEACHER

A significant feature in a successful mentoring scheme is likely to be the quality of the relationship between mentor and protégé – this will inevitably involve issues of hierarchy, confidentiality, trust and openness, and matching or selection. The processes involved appear to identify necessary and distinctive management and staff development needs, and make a real contribution towards meeting them.

An effective induction programme can help protégés to:

- develop an understanding of their organisation
    - its systems and structure;
    - its values and ethos;
    - its politics.
- clarify their new job and role;

- make relationships within their organisation more quickly;
- access the hierarchy of their new organisation.

Mentors have been used effectively in all these ways in induction programmes for new headteachers, lecturers new to Higher and Further Education institutions, teachers in their probationary year and as part of Articled and Licensed Teacher Schemes.

Headteachers new in post experience an acute sense of the importance of their new organisation's immediate history. The systems and structures of an organisation may, on the surface, appear easy to understand, but the underlying principles and the values they evidence are far less obvious. Just what messages are transmitted by following certain procedures, the effect they are having on staff and pupils and what they reveal about the previous headteacher's management style, are all underlying factors which need to be understood by new headteachers. In many cases this growing awareness of their institution is enabled for new headteachers by using an experienced headteacher colleague as a mentor to help interpret the clues they pick up in the early days of their new job. One new head said of his mentor that he appreciated having 'someone to contact when it got really bad,' while another found 'the mentor extended my thinking at different levels' and a third said the mentor helped 'make sense of the clues from staff, children and parents about my school, its history and culture'.

For teachers in their first year, the mentor plays a very different role. People starting out on a career in teaching need to establish themselves in their new school, forming relationships initially with teachers in the same department or section of the school and subsequently with increasing numbers of colleagues across the organisation. Mentors can provide invaluable assistance in providing access to a whole range of different people who for one reason or another can make the probationer's first year that much easier. Access to resources, support and advice are essential to help first year teachers settle into their new environment.

If mentoring can ease the entry of probationers to the school as an organisation, it can also help initial trainees acquire the knowledge and skills necessary for effective classroom teaching. Graduates can elect to train for teaching through the Articled Teacher Scheme in which mentors are used as role models. Through the scheme trainees work as apprentices, learning alongside their mentors. Understanding of the job is paramount, with learning about children and the curriculum (including development, planning, delivery, monitoring and assessment) seen as central aspects of their training.

Whether as part of a staff development or an induction programme, the use of a mentoring system provides access to an individual, supportive relationship in what can sometimes be a strange and daunting situation. In any organisation, a person can identify a circle of professional contacts/colleagues with whom he or she works. Within that group individuals may consider themselves lucky to have someone other than their line manager with whom they can discuss any problems or difficulty. Indeed in many organisations people who are perceived to have 'problems' are often seen as someone to avoid or are thought of as not being 'up to the job'. How much more effective might a person become working in an organisation which attempts, through an effective mentor system, to provide for more than people's professional needs, and by so doing recognises the worth of each individual?

## A MENTORING SYSTEM FOR STAFF DEVELOPMENT

Mentoring systems for staff development are those where everyone, except teachers in their first year of practice, are designated both mentor to someone else, and protégé (ie have someone as their mentor). This support pattern for staff development formalises what originated as a spontaneous, powerful chemistry between two people (what Collin calls the 'love-match' or 'essential' mentoring) into a scheme for the benefit of all individuals *and* the organisation (the 'arranged marriage' or 'instrumental' mentoring) (Collin, 1988).

If the system is to work, senior management must both be involved and be seen to give it high priority. They must offer training opportunities to teachers to become better mentors and facilitate developmental opportunities (which don't have to be secondments on courses). Time has to be allocated to the process. A local school spends one hour every three weeks at a time mutually convenient to both parties. On such a time basis this means each member of staff will be able to talk to his or her mentor every six weeks (or once per half term).

Our own experience suggests that staff are more likely to set targets and change their behaviour as a result of feedback and discussion from a peer and mentor than from their line manager who may be distanced from the situation within which they work. When used as part of an organisation's staff development programme, mentoring will provide protégés with:

- opportunities for meaningful feedback on performance;
- opportunities for greater effectiveness in classroom/workplace;
- opportunities to observe others as role models in the classroom or in general management activities;

- personal support.

The use of a mentor from within the organisation to support a peer colleague's appraisal can help to ensure that the self-review and task-observation elements of the appraisal process are more rigorous and professionally challenging. The mentor provides a view of a colleague's practice which is based on deep insights into his or her work and thus enhances the level of feedback available. The line manager to whom both parties are accountable, complements the appraisals by ensuring that targets are set and that identified development needs are met. In a management context, this dialogue between mentor and appraisee can be effectively extended to consider the appraisee's competence in areas where he or she may have a management responsibility. Through support of this nature, it is possible to ensure that the appraisal process identifies development opportunities more closely matched to individuals' needs than would a purely line-managed system.

## MENTORING AND THE 'LEARNING SCHOOL'

Mentoring is a high-risk activity. Established in organisations which strive to be 'caring communities' it can and should enhance the development of everyone in that organisation. Within the school development plan high priority is given to caring for and developing children, but the support and learning needs of staff colleagues should not be ignored. Mentoring provides a scheme whereby both the mentor and the protégé (and most staff play both roles) can work together to build what Pedler et al. (1989) call 'The Learning Company', ie 'an organisation which facilitates the learning of all of its members and continuously transforms itself.' Such organisations:

a) have a climate in which individual members are encouraged to learn and to develop their full potential;
b) extend this learning culture to include customers (pupils?), suppliers (parents?) and other significant stakeholders (governors and community) wherever possible;
c) make human resource development strategy central to business policy;
d) have a continuous process of organisational transformation harnessing the fruits of individual learning.

## WHAT'S IN THE SYSTEM FOR MENTORS?

So what is in it for the mentors? What do mentors get out of a system which appears time consuming, difficult to implement successfully without training and as yet largely without credibility?

Much will depend on how seriously schools take the notion of staff development. Current thinking in the management of successful or excellent organisations puts great emphasis on the support and development of the organisations' greatest asset, namely the staff. Any worthwhile staff development policy must acknowledge:

- every member of staff's entitlement to development;
- how people learn and develop best;
- that staff development must involve continuous support.

To be a mentor is to contribute to one's own professional development:

1. Helping others to reflect on their practice must be beneficial to oneself. It is difficult not to question your own practice when you are discussing the knowledge, skills or attitudes possessed by others. In trying to diagnose the practice of others, you have to relate what you observe to your own experience and behaviour and thereby try to make sense of them before discussing alternatives.
2. After questioning your own practice there must follow the challenge of doing something to improve it. Often in trying to help others you get insight into your own needs, which acts as a spur to further action – possibly with the aid of your own mentor later.
3. Specific skills are required for successful mentoring. Developing those skills (eg listening, giving feedback, observing practice, coaching, counselling, motivating, diagnosing performance, etc) can only help enhance performance in other areas of your work.

Schools probably have the necessary knowledge and expertise among their staff to deliver training programmes for skill enhancement in most of the areas needed. Delivery of such INSET on site is itself valuable staff development for those involved – for both provider and trainee.

4. Mentor status can enhance the self-esteem, self-confidence and self-image of those acting in that capacity. Having some responsibility for the development of others can be a satisfying and rewarding experience, providing it is handled sensitively and professionally.

A word of warning: helping others when they may have problems can arouse mixed feelings and emotions. It is surely better, however, for people to share their misgivings, doubts, worries and anxieties about their practice with sympathetic colleagues than to soldier on alone with all the attendant dangers of succumbing to the symptoms and effects of stress.

5. Role modelling and helping others develop by example ensures you think carefully about your own practice before demonstrating it in the company of others. Knowing your protégé is to be visiting your classroom tomorrow might makes you think a little harder about your own performance.

## ISSUES FOR CONSIDERATION

Schools which decide to explore the mentoring approach to their staff development strategies are likely to find the following issues will need addressing in the short to medium term:

- the method of selection or allocation of mentors and protégés;
- training and development needs of mentors, as mentors;
- the agreement of standards for minimum levels of entitlement in a mentoring system;
- the establishment of valid and realistic ways of costing the system;
- the precise ways in which mentoring is related to the introduction and operation of the school's appraisal system;
- ways of handling the likely affective issues, the 'feelings' aspect of such ways of close working, and some of the related issues such as confidentiality, resource levels, and staff changes.

The more effective systems using mentoring as and for staff development seem to involve a cyclical pattern, linked with the school and staff development cycles, with a triangle of staff – the protégé, the mentor, and the appraiser – in a complex and delicate balance of development and change. Successful operation of the system can bring the activity of staff development into greater harmony with the activity of pupil and student development which is the heart of the school's purpose.

## REFERENCES

Collin A. (1988). 'Mentoring', *Industrial and Commercial Training*. March/April 1988.
Pedler, M., Boydell, T., and Burgoyne, J. (1989). 'Towards the Learning Company', *Management Education and Development*. vol. 20(1).

# Index

# Index

mentoring
  benefits of 31–2, 93–5, 166,
    178–80
  in collaborative teaching 134–9
  context of 23–4
  contract for 60–61
  difficulties in 52–3
  flexibility in 77
  in-house mentoring 146–9, 156–9
  the learning cycle and mentoring
    174
  models of 21–2
  as needs analysis 74–81
  payment for 127
  professionalism in 60
  skills of 85–95, 104–11
  system 22
  teachers' commitment to 30–32
  teachers' experience of 52–4
  teachers' views of 30–31, 46–51
  team mentoring 146–7
  as theorising 66–9
  whole school approach to *see*
    school

needs analysis
  as generic skill 86
  on Licensed Teacher Scheme
    74–81
negotiation in mentoring 87–8
North of England Conference 17

observation
  limitations of 165–6
  by trainee 53, 90
  of trainee 48, 90–92
Open University 'Frameworks for
  Teaching' (EP228) 157

reflection, context of 109–10
resourcing
  of in-house INSET 151–2
  of school-based training 32–3

school
  climate for training 83–4, 144–6
  involvement in training 56, 63, 72,
    79, 83–4, 128, 146–8
  the 'mentoring school' 152–3, 178
  suitability for training 113
school-based training
  benefits to teachers 128
  difficulties of 131
  evaluation of 163–5
  political influence on 15–18
  professional influence on 14–15
  reasons for 13–14
senior management
  role in innovating 148
  role in training 33–5, 63, 72–3, 83,
    93–5
skills of mentoring 85–95
staff development 63, 73, 93–5,
  152–3, 177–8
supervision
  as distinct from mentoring 37–8,
    63
  skills of 104–11

target setting as mentoring skill 92
theory
  as goal of mentoring 66–9
  need for in training 14–15
  in relation to practice 167–70
training institution
  mentors' knowledge of 70–71
  relationship to school 15–16,
    19–40, 63–4
  role in training 39–40, 63–4
training programme
  as developmental 61–3, 78
  for licensed teacher 76
  as 'survival package' 61–2

wider professional role 51, 62–3